PAT *and* ROALD

PAT

by BARRY FARRELL

and ROALD

RANDOM HOUSE : *New York*

First Printing

9 8 7 6 5 4 3 2

 Published in the United States by Random House, Inc., New York, and simultaneously in Canada by Random House of Canada Limited, Toronto.

Library of Congress Catalog Card Number: 68–28556

Manufactured in the United States of America by Kingsport Press, Inc., Kingsport, Tennessee

Book design by Mary M. Ahern

Title page by Susan Bishop

For Marcia

PAT *and* ROALD

1

SURELY this was an incredible fluke in a city the size of Los Angeles: the ambulance men who had come to take Pat home from the hospital were the same pair who had brought her there a month to the day before. Roald was intensely pleased to see them again, and he greeted them like old squadron mates or school friends. They were fine young fellows, real professionals. He reckoned that there must be thousands of ambulance men in a place as vast and as violent as L.A.—the traffic accidents alone! So it was marvelous that these two random witnesses to the worst moments should now reappear for the unexpected best, the homeward leg of a round trip that they, as tough-minded professionals, must have doubted would ever take place.

The ambulance men stood just inside the door to Pat's room, grinning and nodding their heads to show that they remembered every detail of the first ride precisely as Roald recounted it to her. Pat loved small marvels, uncanny twists, any coincidence, so Roald went to elaborate lengths to describe the miracle of drawing the same lot twice from the vast white army of ambulances tearing through the streets of the city, a siren always heard screaming in all directions. Propped up in bed, Pat smiled warmly all around and appeared to understand: this was the same two men? The ambulance men beamed down on her.

They seemed painted with perpetual rosy grins, these two. It was probably embarrassment, that mixture of pride and embarrassment so typical of Americans when they happen to cross the path of a movie star, regardless of the occasion. Still, they couldn't have been smiling the first time he saw them. They had entered the house like athletes, racing up the stairs with their oxygen cylinder, working over Pat with an efficiency that was really controlled panic, then lifting her and carrying her, bound with a blanket to a chair, down to their wheeled stretcher in a gliding lock step that wouldn't have roused a sleeping child. Obviously they hadn't smiled; it would have been grotesque; he would have remembered. Perhaps they made a point of radiating encouragement when they took people home from the hospital, just as they were determined not to grin when they picked them up.

No tiny refinement or perfected act of kindness would have surprised Roald any more. Along with all the worry and fatigue and the still-unknown consequences of this epic hospital month, the experience had forced Roald to revise his opinion of American medicine. He had spent years honing his attack on the avarice of American doctors, the commercial inhumanity of American hospitals, the really criminal stupidity of American nurses. It was one of his favorite routines when dining with Americans—especially American doctors. Naturally, he had not been able to avoid meeting the occasional doctor whose example seemed to prove him wrong; this only accounted for a few grudging parentheses in an otherwise splendid argument.

But this UCLA Medical Center in Westwood either belonged to a sphere of special excellence or else had to be taken as an endorsement for the superequipped and superefficient American style of hospital medicine that Roald instinctively disliked. The place was like a battleship, what with all its gadgetry and bells. But the staff was helpful and friendly, and everyone moved at a purposeful clip that made Roald feel a sense of trusting security he knew he might well have wished for back home in England. His gratitude took all the sting out of the few complaints he had permitted himself, and he reported them to the staff apologetically, as if he were passing on someone else's small idea. And in fact he had no real complaints. Everything had gone miraculously well.

✿

The first miracle had been getting through to Charlie so quickly. By the peculiar logic of irony, this was a miserable kind of miracle, for if a speeding taxicab had not struck his infant son Theo four years before in New York, Roald surely would not have made a point of always having handy the home telephone number of the best neurosurgeon available. No, it was no accident that Roald consorted so much with neurosurgeons. And however unrewarding it was to think in these terms, it was nonetheless true that if his son had not been so direly punished, his wife would now be dead. Or would she? Had the minutes been that crucial?

February 17, 1965—the day of the stroke—had been a very long one for Pat. She had left home—their rented house in Pacific Palisades—at six o'clock in the morning, and it was nearly time for the children's supper when she returned. There might have been some strain, some tension, because the film she was working in was two weeks late getting started, and Pat was worried that the delay would make it painfully evident that she was pregnant before the movie was finished. But then the shooting began, three days of it, and Pat's high spirits returned. The film was a kind of Chinese Western, *Seven Women,* with Pat starring in the role of a medical missionary who scandalizes her Christian sisters with the same worldly morality that later allows her to save them all by sacrificing herself to the ravages of a Mongol barbarian—or something like that. It was a good part, and Pat was happy to be in a picture directed by John Ford and including in the cast such old and favored friends as Mildred Dunnock, Eddie Albert and Margaret Leighton.

She must have told the story about the donkey first thing upon coming home that night. Sarah, the children's nurse, was there, and so was Angela Kirwan, a pretty young girl they had brought with them from Great Missenden, their village in England; she had offered to do the cooking in exchange for the trip to America. The family was getting to be quite an entourage, almost a tribe. Tessa, eight; Theo, four and a half; and Ophelia, not yet a year old; Angela and Sarah; Pat and Roald: only seven, yet Roald later remembered thinking of his prodigy as Pat told about riding the burro on the set. He was savoring the sheer size and weight of this international caravan of which he was master, conductor, ticket agent and porter, savoring also Pat's little story and the way she told it. When she is elated like this, he thought, she becomes more lovely than ever. Her movements quicken, her voice becomes slightly deeper, and a spark of excitement dances very slowly in the exact center of the pupil of each eye.

Tessa and Theo pressed for details: What donkey? What *is* a donkey? How high? How fast? The story ran on until Pat reminded herself that they had a dinner date that night. Tessa asked her mother if she would bathe her in the big bathroom off the master bedroom. Pat agreed and the two of them went upstairs together. Don-mini (as they called Ophelia) was already asleep in her crib; Sarah was bathing Theo in the other bathroom. Roald stayed with the others, chatting with Angela's boy friend, a young actor who, when pressed, turned out to be a garage mechanic. Two weeks in California, and she had a boy friend already. Roald disapproved. Now Angela wanted to go for an evening swim. The sun sparkled silver on the swimming pool. It wasn't bad to be in California, especially in February, when the weather could be so miserable at home.

Roald wandered upstairs, bored with baiting the actor. He found Pat standing in the bedroom, swaying, wincing in pain and pressing the palm of her hand against her left temple.

"I've got the most awful pain right here," she said. "I think there's something wrong."

Roald went over to her. His heart had been pounding audibly, it seemed, from the instant he entered the room.

"I've been seeing things," Pat said.

"What sort of things?"

"I don't know. I can't remember."

Roald was deathly afraid. Did he tremble? Later he thought that he had. She went to the bed and lay down. Roald stood next to her.

"The pain is terrible," she said and closed her eyes.

"Is it only in one place?"

"Yes . . . here . . . right here," and as she spoke he knew, knew beyond doubt that life would never be the same, knew that a new and terrible calamity had struck. Pat was dying —he felt it, didn't question it, acted, moved fast, lost no time to panic. "Don't move," he said and raced to his study where Charlie's number was tacked to the wall above his desk. He snatched the scrap of paper off the wall and ran back to the bedroom. Pat's eyes were open now. He picked up the phone and dialed: busy. He dialed again. Again busy. Again he dialed. This time it rang and Charlie answered.

"Charlie, it's Roald."

"Hi. How are you?" Roald could hear Charlie's children playing in the background, laughing and shouting.

"This is an emergency."

Charlie spoke sharply to his children and their laughter stopped abruptly. "Yes, go on," he said.

"It's Pat."

"You mean Theo—"

"No. I mean Pat. She's having terrific pain in her left temple and her eyes aren't clear."

"Is her neck rigid?"

"No. I don't know. Not yet." As he spoke, Pat's mouth fell open and her eyes closed slowly.

"She's losing consciousness . . ."

"Okay. Here's what we do—"

"Now she's vomiting. Can you come at once?"

"No. I'll meet you at the hospital. I'll send an ambulance. It's quicker. I'll be there when you arrive."

"Where?"

"UCLA. Emergency entrance."

And thus the two ambulance men had arrived in record time. Roald's first awareness of them came from the sound of their siren, distant at first, then drawing nearer, summoning and confirming his grief and fear, screaming finally—screaming right past the house and on up the block, terrorizing the children. Tessa! Poor Tessa, who had been there on the street corner to watch the taxi slam her infant brother into the side of a bus, and then, two years later, had seen the ambulance men come for Olivia, her elder sister, never to bring her back again. Tessa, cold and bewildered in the bathtub with the siren crying in the street. Roald felt a flash of real fury. He shouted to the actor—go out in the street and flag those fools down. Sarah helped Tessa out of the bath, and the little girl padded damply down the silent hall to her room.

Roald held a teaspoon wrapped in a handkerchief between Pat's teeth to stop her from biting her tongue, thinking that she was so critically ill that it wouldn't make much difference whether she bit it or not. But what else was there to do? He had searched his mind a hundred times for some omission, some trick of first aid that might make a difference.

There was nothing to do but wait and hold the absurd teaspoon, until he heard the hurried steps of the ambulance men bounding up the stairs—good men, other hands to help.

Pat had regained consciousness, but her memory was gone. "Who is in this house?" she said. "What are the names of the people in this house, please? Who *are* they all? You must tell me the names."

"You mean the children's names?"

"Yes! Yes! The children's names."

But the force of things overcame any chance to talk. Pat's eyes were losing focus; the ambulance men were securing her to the chair. They eased her out of the room and Roald hurried ahead to guide them down the stairs and through the house. Then they were off, holding the siren until they were clear of the house, then letting it unwind with a mounting shriek that filled his ears and trilled against his effort to be calm all the way into the hospital. The ride took less than ten minutes; it was barely a half-hour since it all had begun.

There had already been two hemorrhages by the time Charlie began his examination; a third, the worst and most massive, struck Pat as she lay unconscious in the x-ray room while the doctors were photographing the arteries of the brain to locate the point of bleeding. The process is exacting: before each x-ray, a radiopaque medium must be injected into the blood stream, which gives the radiologist seven or eight seconds to take his picture. Since so many are required, the team worked on Pat for three hours before the job was done. Then Charlie called Roald into the viewing room to look at the x-rays.

One wall was almost entirely covered with radiographs of

the inside of Pat's skull, eerie chalk visions with the arteries showing in white, the brain itself in filigreed gray. There, repeated from all angles, in close-up and perspective, there in the center of it all was a white spot, a dot the size of a dime ("The aneurysm," Charlie said; Roald had heard the term). An aneurysm is a spot of weakness in an artery wall. It balloons, stretches, extends until the arterial tissue is gossamer-thin. Then it tears without warning and begins to leak, sometimes squirting blood into surrounding tissues under very high pressure. The stream of escaping blood can do great damage if the aneurysm happens to occur in the brain, where the tissue is gelatinous and easily destroyed. And Pat's aneurysm lay in a region where it menaced lobes that govern word recognition and speech, as well as many movements of the right side. Charlie sketched out the problem in detail, locating the break at the conjunction of the internal carotid artery and the posterior communicating artery, a likely spot for trouble, the site of many aneurysms. "Her condition is very critical," he said.

"Are you going to operate?" Roald asked.

"I doubt she would survive an operation."

"What will happen if you don't?"

"If I don't, then she is certain to die."

"In that case, you must operate."

"Yes. All right. But please don't be too hopeful."

"How long will it take?"

"I don't know. Maybe five hours. Maybe seven. I'll send word to you as I go along."

Then he was out in the hall for the all-night vigil. He waited first in the corridor, then in a roomful of fathers-to-be, then back to the corridor. He tried to resist the thought that he had seen the last of Pat, Pat as she had always been, funny and beautiful, lively, loving Pat—how could it be true? And how had he told the children? He was astonished not to recall. He ought to remember exactly how they had looked when he broke the news to them, the frozen moment that stays in the mind like a snapshot, Theo in his pyjamas, Tessa's trembling lip. But he simply could not remember He knew he had discussed the problem of telling them with Millie Dunnock when he called her from the hospital.

"Do the children know?"

"Yes, of course—that something's wrong. They heard the siren. They know Pat's sick."

Later he remembered the conversation, remembered thinking that you can never tell how deeply things affect children; you don't know how badly they're shaken. They get anxious, of course, whenever anything happens to the family. They get anxious for themselves; they think they're next on the list. The thought came to him that someone else should tell the children. They would need him badly now, and it would be easier for them if he could remain a solid pillar of safety, untouched by the shock of the news. But that was Millie's idea, not his. She had offered to spare him the pain of explaining things to the children—something he would never have thought of on his own. Perhaps he had let Millie talk to them early the next morning; he couldn't recall.

It was seven in the morning before he saw Pat. He had waited for an hour by the elevator doors before they slid open to reveal Pat on a rolling bed, her head bound in a huge turban, her face pale and still. They moved quickly, wheeling her past him and down the hall to the Intensive

Care Unit. Then Charlie appeared, looking desperately tired and worn.

"She's a strong girl," he said.

"Will she live?"

"I don't know. All I can tell you is . . . it was a good operation."

"Good operation"—the words stood out like a beacon against the haze and gloom of that night. He lived by those words for the next two weeks, forcing himself to believe them and not lose faith in them while the coma held Pat in a sleep so deep and distant that no matter how he studied her face or begged her to hear him, she seemed more dead than alive.

Roald managed to coax all the details of the operation out of Charlie. The head had been shaved and the incision traced in an arc above the left temple; the skull was opened with burr holes connected by the Gigli saw, laying back a trap door that gave entry to the brain. Blood clots were found and removed inside the dura, the parchmentlike covering of the brain. Then a cut was made into the temporal lobe to remove another large clot. The temporal lobe was then lifted away to expose the aneurysm, which was closed with two V-shaped silver clips long enough to occlude it. Finally a stainless-steel clip was fastened over the base of the aneurysm and sprayed with a plastic adhesive to hold it in place. Throughout the operation the landmarks of the brain had been difficult to identify because of massive bleeding. The third cranial nerve, which controls movements of the eyes, appeared to be intact.

The coma made day and night identical, for Roald as well as for Pat. He drove back and forth from the house in Pacific

Palisades to the hospital so many times every day that he often arrived at his destination unaware of having made the trip. His friendship with Charlie deepened on the strength of very few words spoken and many looks exchanged. He felt tremendously heartened at the very sight of Charlie; even when the doctor's mood did nothing to confirm his optimism, it was reassuring just to watch him as he examined Pat, testing, listening, looking for any sign of change. Charlie was unquestionably a top neurosurgeon by any standard, and beyond that he was a genuine friend. Roald's feelings for him were not in the least bit complicated by the debt of thanks he owed him and could never quite repay. He admired Charlie and he liked him—here he was, after all, calling him Charlie!

And Jean. Jean Alexander belonged to a rare breed of nurse. Her competence and her rapport with patients were enough to make her exceptional, even among the elite corps of nurses assigned to the Intensive Care Unit. But she was also an unusually sensitive girl who had understood Roald's need to know every detail of Pat's condition and the function of every drug and treatment given her.

Roald's sisters often remarked that he would have made a splendid doctor. It was a cliché about him, a cliché he never disputed. He could never have been a country G.P. tooling around the villages with aspirin and tongue depressors. But a heart specialist or a neurosurgeon, something like that would have made for a marvelous life. He often regretted the way his education had gone; imagine, preparing for a career in commerce!

Luckily, writing had saved him from wasting his life as a business dog, but his affinity for medicine was fed only by a

Mittyish capacity for fantasy until the family's luck turned sour and he saw no choice but to delve into it in earnest. Still, long before he saw his first craniotomy he had written a short story that was, neurologically speaking, impeccable. In "William and Mary" a dying philosopher agrees to have his brain kept alive in a basin after his death, with a heart machine pumping in the sustaining blood and one eye floating on the surface of the sterile solution, permitting the philosopher to read his daily copy of the *Times* long after his body is buried. Fantastic, of course, yet not so fantastic. All the details were sound and true. They were even doing the operation on chimps now, or so Roald had read. Minus the floating eye, of course.

Then, with Theo's accident Roald's real introduction to the life of the brain began. The blow to Theo's head had shattered his skull like porcelain, and from the multiple injuries to his brain he developed hydrocephalus. The treatment for this illness consists of inserting a tube, or shunt, running from one ventricle of the brain down into some region of the body where the excess fluid can be absorbed—the heart, for example. It is a brutal kind of therapy, but there was no choice. Without the shunt, cerebrospinal fluid accumulates in the skull, causing enlargement of the head and compression of the brain, and ultimately bringing mental retardation, blindness and, usually, death. The shunt relieves all the symptoms of hydrocephalus by carrying the fluid off to the heart or pleura or a kidney, but its life span is very short. The tubing blocks or the miniature valve inside it either jams on a tiny morsel of brain tissue or else the whole device becomes the focus of infection. If any one of these things occurs the shunt must be replaced, and in Theo's case it had to be replaced eight times in thirty months. Each time, he would grow drowsy, run a fever and throw fits; three times he went blind. And each time there would be another operation, another trauma in a tiny life once described by Roald in a classic paragraph:

> It is a long fight and a hard one to keep a hydrocephalic child going. The shunt blocks, the pressure builds, the eyes go groggy. Then comes the drive to the hospital, the walk through the snow (it was always snowing) to the hospital entrance, the swift elevator ride to the neurosurgical floor, and suddenly there you are again, standing in the pale yellow corridor with the child in your arms, handing him over, consigning him, trusting him to the ruthless but precise alchemy of the neurosurgeons: the subdural taps, the lumbar punctures, the manometers, the myelograms, and finally, inevitably, comes the operation itself. When it is over, you go into the ward and you see upon the bed a great turban of white bandages, and below it a small pale face and two huge blue eyes that are wide open, desolate, bewildered. The eyes look at you, and they are saying, "Why did you let them do this to me again?"

In his fury against the repeated invasions of Theo's brain, Roald determined to try to make a better shunt. He remembered having met a mechanical genius named Stanley Wade while flying model airplanes in a field near Amersham fifteen years before. Roald's planes were as graceful as gulls, and big enough to be convincing as they roared in circles overhead. But Stanley's planes were powered by tiny hand-built engines of his own make and design. It was a happy coincidence that Stanley's business should be the manufacture of hydraulic precision pumps in a factory Roald passed every morning when he drove Tessa to school in nearby High Wycombe.

The problem of the shunt was a question of precision hydraulics on the smallest workable scale. A miniaturist at heart, Stanley was obviously the man for the job, and he agreed at once to give it a try.

Taciturn and shy, Stanley gave the project his full attention, letting his business run itself while he studied all varieties of shunts and pumps, determining that their use and application in the treatment of hydrocephalus depended upon a science composed of "brute force and bloody ignorance." He worked up improved models in a home machine shop equipped with tools as fine as a jeweler's, rejecting one after another when they failed to respond to the subtle ranges of pressure the shunt required. Roald served as corresponding secretary, liaison and translator between Stanley and Kenneth Till, a London neurosurgeon who had been recruited as consultant. It took three years but finally they had it, a puzzle solved in thirteen pieces, a sequence of valves and screens and washers encased in a flexible tube one inch and a half long and with a smaller circumference than a drinking straw, a one-way system that would allow cerebrospinal fluid to drip freely away from the zone of pressure in the skull, at the same time permitting the wearer to turn an occasional cartwheel without fear of the returning tide, an almost perfect little machine, to be sold around the world for less than a third the price of shunts that worked less well. It was an important triumph for the three of them, the Wade-Dahl-Till Valve, now in use on four continents, a lifesaving, mind-saving device carried under the scalps of many hundreds of rescued children; something to be proud of, intensely. Roald tried to recall an occasion in his life that had rewarded him as deeply: winning his wings in the RAF, the publication of his first story, his first book? But there was nothing there to match the shunt.

The work had given Roald a kind of apprenticeship in neurology: he had read a great deal, had watched operations and spent many evenings talking with Kenneth, and he had learned enough about the life of the brain to appreciate the marvel of this boundless universe. Now, sitting at Pat's bedside, he could visualize the soft coils, twin snails lying side by side in the darkness of the skull, and he knew the infinite delicacy and complexity of the mushroom substance that was truth and beauty and all else that defined a human life. His knowledge had not been ordered into real understanding; isolated facts plucked strings of wonderment in his imagination until his thoughts converged in a feeling close to awe. It seemed bitter knowledge now—it was monstrous, horrible, a plague upon him. And yet he could not shake his fascination for this labyrinthine terrain flooded and torn in his wife as it had been in his son. He looked at Pat not only in sorrow but also with interest, excitement, a sense of adventure coming on.

Sorrow, or depression, was the most manageable of his feelings. He despised finding any trace of it in himself or in his friends. Depression was proof that you were weakening. It was appalling how easily people let themselves slip into it, like children pulling blankets over their heads. Roald refused to indulge in it.

Roald was convinced of it: staying alive meant trusting yourself in bad moments, going at life as if it were a horse to be broken. That was better than all the sympathy and grief you could shower on people who were suffering. He knew that his bedside manner did not exactly correspond to everyone's idea of how he should behave, with Pat in such a pitiful condition. He was too active, he supposed—too positive. Some of her visitors seemed openly upset at his efforts to get through to her; he could feel them straining against the impulse to tell him to quit hounding her, to let her have some peace. But this was not peace—this was war, and you could only fight it with all your resources. So he sorted the mail and read it and answered a very good part of it. He cleaned up the litter, gave away flowers, emptied ashtrays, interviewed passing doctors and nurses, held Pat's hand, talked his head off, searched for any sign of returning awareness.

He was acting on pure instinct. He had no idea whether one should speak low or loud or not at all in the ear of one's comatose wife. Nor did he stop to wonder. He simply acted out of some natural spring of feeling, following the impulse to call her back by whatever means he could. After the miracle had happened, he was not certain what he had done. Had he shouted? Shouted in her ear? He could scarcely imagine doing it, yet vaguely he had a recollection of shouting, "Pat, this is Roald. Roald, Pat. Tessa says hello. Theo says hello. Don-mini says hello. Pat, it's Roald."

Yes, probably he had shouted. He knew that he had slapped Pat's cheeks and peeled her eyelids back—perhaps a shade more often than a medical man might have done. Strictly speaking. The doctors performed these acts with an enviable diagnostic flair, and Roald had been careful to observe how they went about it. But at times he had also detected in them a trace of mortal anguish, some barely visible sign that the doctor suffered too and longed for the coma to end.

Because a coma is purgatory. You cannot share it. What you have to go by are the "vital signs," so-called: heart, pulse, respiration, the look of the eyes. But even if all are strong and certain, they are sometimes not so vital; rather, they are like stars over ocean blackness—whimpers and flickers, nothing more. Pat lay on a cooling mattress, a bed of ice to forestall edema in the damaged brain. She had a tube in her nose for feeding, a tracheostomy for breathing, a catheter for urine, restraining straps on her left arm and leg. Her skin had lost much of its turgor, and she made no voluntary movements. The coma was lasting too long. He knew that his optimism surpassed what the doctors thought wise, and he knew they were concerned for his own well-being. They were preparing him for the worst, just as Charlie had done from the beginning. Pat's chances were poor; he knew it.

Roald was living at such an extreme of fatigue and worry that in some respects he was numb. A great many nuances were no doubt escaping his notice. He had spent hundreds of hours simply staring at Pat, studying her face, seeing her and thinking about her in a way he had rarely done before. He saw things in her face that he had not discovered in twelve years of marriage. Often he woke with a start to find he had been sleeping in his chair.

Then it happened: Pat began to stir, unmistakably. At first there was no more than the merest answering squeeze in her fingers, a tremble at the tips. But soon she began to move around on the bed, and her left hand had to be tied down to prevent it from reaching up and pulling out the feeding tube or the tube that served her tracheotomy. The squeezes grew stronger and more responsive as the days passed, and then one day her right eye popped open and stared back at him for fully five seconds before dropping shut again.

It was a marvelous thing to witness—the slow, mysterious recovery of an injured brain—but it was also clear that no one else made quite so much of these signs of life. One night, jubilant over some frail signal, Roald ran into Charlie in the hospital parking lot. "She's going to live!" he exclaimed. "I'm absolutely sure of it."

"Yes, she is," Charlie answered. "But I'm not sure whether or not I've done her a favor."

One afternoon while Roald stood by the window smoking, he heard a rustle that caused him to turn around and discover that Pat had her eyes fully open and was reaching out to him. It took a second for the image to register. Then he was across the room, calling for Jean to come witness the miracle, fumbling with his cigarette to free his hand for Pat. Then the thought struck him that she was reaching out for a puff. It's the cigarette, he thought—she wants a drag! She wants a drag on the cigarette! His excitement and laughter stole the whole moment of consciousness, and Pat was asleep again before he could respond: just as well not to have to turn her down on her first returning wish. But it was Pat, all right, waking from her coma with all her vices intact. And if all her vices, then all her virtues as well. Lingering doubts fled. If Pat wanted a cigarette first thing on waking, then nothing very serious could be wrong with her.

Her eyes started opening together soon, and within a few days she managed an occasional smile. Her smile was marvelously eloquent. It was like a flower coming into bud and blossom, revealing itself in leaps of life and growth. He and Jean basked in it, grinning back like idiots. He brought friends into the ward to see her, and Pat rewarded them all with a smile. Katie Marlowe, Lillian Hellman, Betsy Drake, Cary Grant, Chloe Carter, Jean Valentine, Sarah, Angela—all old friends of Pat's, and Pat seemed to know them all.

And then she spoke. Jean was singing as she tidied up around the bed, and suddenly Pat chimed in, just for a single word. After twenty-two days of silence she finally uttered a word, but nothing came after it. Roald knew that by some bizarre cerebral decree, the lyrics of songs are stored in a part of the brain that has nothing to do with spontaneous speech or word recognition. He had heard of cases in which stroke victims survived with vocabularies that consisted of nothing but curses and songs. But it was something wonderful all the same, a new miracle, and in the days that followed, it expanded until she could join in on songs she had learned twenty years before, the words all there along with the tune: "Jimmy Crack Corn," "Down in the Valley," "Where Did You Get That Hat?" Jean searched her memory for more and more songs, and Roald was astounded at the number she knew. The girl was a walking anthology of unimagined Americana. Roald suggested a few songs himself, songs he remembered hearing Pat sing to the children. But if Jean didn't know them by their titles they were lost, since Roald could not be made to sing or even hum. Singing in public, even therapeutically, was something quite beyond him.

Pat loved and trusted Jean almost as a child would, and in these last hospital days her looks and gestures conveyed the anxiety she felt to be leaving her. Roald had been quick to insist that Jean come by the house as often as she could, and he drew her a map of the route from Westwood out to Pacific Palisades to make sure that she would take him up on it. But this was really more for Pat's sake than for Jean's, and Roald had puzzled for days over how to thank her properly.

Finally, on an impulse that came to him one of the endless afternoons by Pat's bedside in the ICU, he invited Jean to come to England for a year and to bring along Gloria, her roommate. At first Jean was incredulous at the prospect of such extravagant good luck—neither she nor Gloria had ever been east of Chicago. She told Roald that she would have to talk it over seriously with Gloria, but it took them not a day to decide that they would go. Their enthusiasm delighted Roald, and he congratulated himself for having hit upon such a fine idea. It would be simple enough to find a spot for them in a good hospital through Kenneth Till, or perhaps through Roald's brother-in-law, Sir Ashley Miles, head of the Lister Institute. But no, Kenneth would be better. Roald hated to ask anything of Ashley. He would ask Kenneth instead. So the only question was the round-trip air fare, and since the project was such a worthy one, he could use the trust fund for that.

Pat's singing was conclusive evidence that neither her voice nor speech mechanism was impaired—and thank God for that. Her voice was the most distinctive thing about her, an instrument she could play to a thousand effects. It was one thing about her people never forgot, her wonderful dark mahogany voice. And from the way her intelligence was rattling the gates of speechlessness, it was obvious that many things had already silted up inside her, waiting to be said. She would roll her eyes like a bound-and-gagged bank clerk in her impatience to be heard, and even with the right side of her face puffed and flaccid with paralysis, she had an arsenal of new frowns and eyebrow archings that arrived on her brow quick as darts and gave her an active place in conversations.

To Roald, it was unmistakably clear that in all essential ways she had survived, along with the child she was carrying. Her eyesight was maddeningly blurred by double vision, but that was said to be transitory, and for the moment a simple eye patch made it easier to bear. The right arm and leg were paralyzed, but exercise and a leg brace would eventually restore them to use. She would have speech and intellectual functioning to recover. The trick now would be in leading her back to the woman she was, teaching her all that she once knew. It was simply a question of work and time.

Covering an eye with her good hand, Pat could make the swimming stop, bringing the room into focus. There by the window sat her husband, going through the mail. Her husband's face was a good face, she thought. Even with both eyes open, spinning like marbles, it seemed, and making the room dip and smear, her husband's face was a good one. Close by the bed, sometimes leaning over her, reading, or sitting there in the sunlight, peeking in at the door, he was . . . her husband. She could not think of his name.

Pat's progress became so swift that she was beginning to lapse into irony and boredom before the doctors could be sure that the seige on her brain had lifted. She had been moved to a room down the hall, and they would come to tickle the soles of her feet with pins and feathers, testing sensation and reflex. Pat's eyes would say yes, yes, of course I feel it—now what? After several days' work she managed to feed herself left-handed; big deal, said the eyes. What mattered to her were the children. She missed them so badly that Roald eventually persuaded himself to smuggle them in to see her one afternoon. Theo smiled shyly at the sight of her, establishing his special understanding of these neurosurgical sufferings, and Tessa smiled for the first time in a month.

From the beginning, Roald had removed most of the flowers from Pat's room, to clear it of their saccharine odor. He didn't want her bedside to look like a Hollywood extravaganza, with the luxurious sprays and bouquets (sent by the secretaries of various moguls and actors and agents) devouring all the oxygen in the air. He must have given away fifty dozen flowers, to Jean or any nurse who happened to be passing by in the corridor, keeping just a few from close friends. He had also held the press at bay, a considerable trick, especially in the first two weeks while Pat was still in a coma and the papers carried nightly bulletins on her condition. She had become a powerful moral instrument in the act of falling ill—a heroine of illness, a most unlikely role for Pat. But there it was to contend with, a new kind of fame far more intense than either of them had known in pursuit of their two careers.

Roald had been surprised at the dramatic play the Los Angeles papers gave the story from the start. "OSCAR WINNER STRICKEN" was the headline that stayed in his mind, if only because it had seemed so startingly inappropriate to the circumstances when he saw it at the hospital an hour or so after the operation: he hadn't thought of Pat as an Oscar winner that night. He read the first dozen or so stories with real interest, discovering that he had been roundly mistaken in his guess that only Los Angeles papers would treat Pat's illness as a page-one calamity. Admittedly, there wasn't a great deal else happening in the world during the first critical days—South Vietnam installed a new Cabinet; Secretary McNamara called for more fallout shelters. Yet the papers all showed genuine devotion to Pat, and through the long string of nights and days when she lay in danger, they continued to print late reports from the hospital in grave little paragraphs marking every stage of the vigil, like puffs of smoke from the Vatican. "ACTRESS FIGHTS FOR LIFE"; "PAT NEAL STILL IN COMA"; "HOPE SEEN FOR STRICKEN STAR." Roald was thankful for the attention, since friends and family all across the country and in England were kept almost as well informed as if he had had the time and will to write them all a letter every day. It didn't matter all that much that the details were often imprecise or simply wrong. Things got sorted out eventually, and the basic reassuring fact was always present—Pat lives. Taken together, these thousands of bold-face bulletins amounted to an overwhelming tribute to Pat. Who could help but be pleased?

But when a fresh batch of news flashes announced Pat's first stirrings and predicted her survival and recovery, Roald began to detect something terribly maudlin in it all. "STRICKEN STAR" was an alliteration that occurred to headline writers with such appalling regularity that they would be slow to abandon it merely because it had ceased to apply, and Roald dreaded the journalistic future if Pat was to become a staple item for the Sunday trade in lugubrious features. He was also faintly tired of seeing the family's misfortunes recounted again and again in the same blunt sequence, reducing the events of a Jobian cycle of years to a clipping no bigger than the weather forecast. He could recite it in his sleep. *Miss Neal has been plagued by tragedy in recent years. Her baby son, Theo, was nearly killed by a taxi in New York in 1960. He has had eight major skull operations. Her eldest child, Olivia, died of the measles two years later. She is married to the English short-story writer, Ronald Dahl.* He had grown so accustomed to reading the same lament for his wife and children that he skimmed over it as if it had nothing whatever to do with him, registering only the faintest twinge of displeasure when the papers called him "Ronald," as they did about half the time.

So the press had promoted Pat from Oscar winner to a more fundamental kind of heroine, a saint of suffering, and although there was no doubt in Roald's mind that she was a very good choice for the honor, it was still a sticky business. He wondered how Pat would take to it when her awareness returned enough to appreciate the change. There were many fine edges of irony in all that had come to her in her long and dangerous sleep. It was already clear that she had no memory of the stroke itself, the pain, the bursting aneurysm, the ambulance ride. Her memory left off when she was strong and well, a late-blooming beauty more convincing in her late thirties than in her glamorous Hollywood twenties, and a far better actress, an actress whose own life had provided a currency that could cover anything dreamed up by scriptwriters. Still, you couldn't have called her great box office—not a superstar, not a big public favorite. The Oscar might have made a subtle difference eventually, but nothing like the great outpouring of affection that was suddenly hers, now that she could neither speak nor walk nor understand it.

Roald reflected that this, too, was an American specialty, this vast sentimental love of the ill that created a folkloric object of pity out of a stricken public personality. The English, perhaps, were the greater hypochondriacs, but the Americans had a positive mania for finding inspiration in someone else's disability, as if illness purified rather than destroyed. Helen Keller was obviously queen of the genre, and the thought of her reminded Roald of a marvelous fight one night in Philadelphia, when the Broadway production of *The Miracle Worker* was out on the road for its trial run. Pat was playing Helen Keller's mother, and to Roald's taste, she was laying it on a bit thick. He disliked the whole spirit of the play profoundly, but as he made his way back to her dressing room he decided to limit himself to a few discreet words in Pat's ear; he respected her talent too much to play at being her drama coach, especially in front of others. Pat must have taken his criticism badly, or else some devilish impulse got the best of him. Before he knew it he was shouting his contempt for actors who would dare approach such a story with self-pity and weakness, and his tone with Pat became so harsh that soon her real tears had replaced the fake ones he was trying to denounce. The director ordered him off the premises as a troublemaker, but not before Roald had already stormed away in righteous disregard of the figure he was cutting. It was a fine old flare-up, all right, and he supposed one really ought to regret such moments. But in the end everyone agreed that the interpretation Pat brought to the role the next night was much more effective. Dignify suffering with restraint and you've got deeper suffering;

people will be willing to suffer with you. Roald had no way of knowing if Pat's performance was faithful to the facts, but it was a style of behavior natural and becoming to her, if not to Helen Keller's mother.

Leaving the hospital turned out a bigger event than Roald had foreseen. There was nothing to do but say good-bye and go, but an hour passed, with the ambulance men standing by while flocks of unfamiliar nurses and nurses's aides stole timidly into the room to draw or open the curtains, fill the thermos jug or, finding it full, empty it and fill it up again. Roald was impatient to get started, but he was charmed by this show of affection for Pat. In all the time she had been a patient there, the staff had given no sign of being aware of who she was outside the hospital. Roald admired them for their restraint; he hated any display of excess emotion, even in sympathy and caring.

Millie Dunnock had joined the leave-taking party in Pat's room, bringing with her a wig which was borrowed from MGM no doubt, for Pat to wear home from the hospital. Motherly Millie. Roald stood by as she fussed with the wig, sliding it back and forth over the stockinette that covered Pat's long scar and the dark infantile fuzz that had grown back since the operation. It was clear from the look in Pat's eyes that she was counting on the wig to do more for her than it could. Jean held up a mirror and Pat clamped her eyes shut in dismay. The wig looked like a banana peel. Millie struggled on.

Now at last they were leaving. Charlie had agreed that getting home would give Pat's morale a great boost, and had arranged for therapy to begin the very next morning. A physical therapist and a speech therapist would be coming for an hour each, every day. The wig was not a success, so Pat left the hospital wearing a kind of turban which, along with her eye patch, made her look like a wounded Turk. A flurry of white-coated arms waved good-bye as the ambulance pulled away from the hospital. Now there would be no siren, Roald thought, just the good ride home.

2

IT WAS well past the children's bedtime, but both Tessa and Theo still could be heard tearing through the upstairs rooms, shrieking with laughter as Sarah plodded miserably after them. Theo's laugh pierced the California plaster in bright little stabs of glee; Tessa's touched notes that drilled through carpet and flooring. Roald twisted in his chair and considered going up to quiet them, but then thought better of it. Only a few days before, Sarah had complained that he was undermining her authority with the children, her soft Scottish burr making the crime sound rather worse than it was—un*derrr*mining au*thurr*ity. Still, he could see that she had a point. He would wait until she had them in bed before going up for the tuck-in.

Angela brought in coffee on a tray and Roald got up to make a last fine adjustment on the television picture. A shade darker, more contrast. Pat sipped steadily from her coffee cup, eyes fixed on the parade of commercials. She had two cigarettes burning at once, one clamped between the fingers that held the cup, the other forgotten in the ashtray next to her. The Oscar show was about to begin.

But for the stroke, Pat would have been part of the show. She had won her Oscar the year before, and tradition required that last year's Best Actress be there to bless this year's Best Actor. She had missed being present to receive her Oscar in 1964, for her role as Alma in *Hud,* because Ophelia's birth had kept her home in England. Now, in bathrobe, head scarf and leg brace, she was missing it again. Audrey Hepburn had flown in from Switzerland to stand in for her.

Roald enjoyed Hollywood as much as Pat did, provided he could keep his British distance. He loved all the machinations, the money, the weave of opposing vanities, the marvelous outpourings of sentiment. "The Hepburn ploy" struck him as a master stroke, and he took great pains to explain it to Pat.

"What we have here, you see, is a complicated Hollywood power play. Now, everyone knows that Julie Andrews is going to get the Oscar for *Mary Poppins.* And Audrey was the one who beat her out for the plum part of the year in *My Fair Lady.* Do you remember how Julie was supposed to be very sad? Her agents must have told her, 'Well, you'll have to be content with this crummy Disney film, but it's a pity you missed the big one, sister.' And the big one came out and then *Poppins* came out, and Andrews stole the Oscar from Hepburn. Do you see? Hepburn wasn't even nominated. And so it's very clever of the *My Fair Lady* boys to get Hepburn out on the rostrum under any guise. Because

Rex Harrison will get Best Actor, and you'll have Harrison and Hepburn in front of the cameras together—a big *My Fair Lady* promotion."

It was hard to tell how much Pat understood. She would nod, smile, make signs of understanding, only to look away in midsentence and forget. The coffee cup, the cigarettes, the sounds of the children, the nonsense collage on television—anything could become a distraction until it wore on too long and something else stole her attention. She had been home from the hospital a month and her progress was amazing. She could move around the house, say at least a dozen words, light her own cigarettes one-handed, even get herself dressed. But her concentration was as fragile as a child's, and even when the whole of her being was alight with fascination, neither she nor the others could count on it to last.

Audrey Hepburn had made her entrance before it quite registered on them that Bob Hope had just finished introducing her. "There! There!" said Pat, pointing sharply to the screen. Ah, yes, the classic Hepburn smile was there in close-up now. Pat bore down to listen and watch, cocking her head to the angle of her eye patch. Obviously still the actress, Roald thought. She may not look it, but she's still an actress to the core. She can hardly wait to hear the mushy things they'll be saying about her.

But the demure little speech was over before they were settled to hear it begin. Audrey Hepburn was handing the Oscar to Rex Harrison, then exiting with a broad valedictory smile that lasted all the way into the wings. Pat pounded the table with her good hand. "God! God! Me! Not me!" It was simple enough for Angela to supply the words she needed: "Are you annoyed because she didn't mention you?"

"Yeah!"

And she was, royally. She glared at the television set, incensed and unbelieving, and she showed not the slightest hint of pleasure when her name was mentioned, after all: "We're all pulling for Pat Neal, who couldn't be here to-night." Pat felt a cold and lonely wrath, a sense of being cheated. The want of words made her fury more intense than if she had been able to speak it out. Neither Roald's loyal invective nor Angela's attempts to find some charitable explanation could do anything to dispel her rage. "Bed?" Roald asked, and Pat sighed yes. There was no consoling her.

Going upstairs, they formed a small procession that moved at a safe geriatric pace, and each of Pat's steps was honored as a mission accomplished. Roald had had to carry Pat up and down the stairs until a few days before, sixteen steps each way, at least four times a day. This was no mean feat even for Roald, who at six feet six and weighing two hundred pounds was remarkably well conditioned from years of heavy-weightlifting prescribed for his war-injured back. For not only did Pat, in her fifth month of pregnancy, weigh over one hundred and forty pounds, but the weakness and rigidity in her right side also made her an exceedingly awkward armful—things kept bumping and spilling. But now, while Pat grasped the banister with her left hand, Angela supported her firmly from the right and Roald followed close behind in case she tumbled backward. With Roald and Angela peering down to find the foot in the shadow of Pat's long bathrobe, making sure it was planted squarely enough to trust for the next plunge upward, they eased their way up to the landing, paused in conquest, then turned down the hall to the bedroom. Angela dashed ahead to open the door and turn back the sheets.

The telephone rang as they reached their goal: a reporter, calling to ask what Miss Neal had thought of the Oscar show. Roald took the phone. "She thought it bloody well stank," he said, and Pat's eyes flashed her vindicating joy. Angela helped her off with the leg brace, a spring-tension stirrup that rose from the heel of a police matron's oxford to a leather collar that fastened just below the knee. Then Roald lifted her smoothly into the center of the bed. She was asleep even before they put out the lights.

Roald went down to his study and placed calls to several friends. His mind was racing and he needed to talk, as if only by hearing himself explain his ideas to his friends could he discover precisely what he thought. His friends were used to such calls—they were his automatic response to all varieties of trouble. It was not so much that he wished to sound alarms or give vent to his anger or ask anyone's advice. It was instead a natural act of intimacy and the mandate of his friendship. Ordinarily Roald's reserve could be all but impenetrable. But when something went wrong the telephone would ring, and there would be Roald, suddenly close and accessible.

In genuine emergencies Roald could not avoid measuring his friends by the way they answered his first call. There were people who would drive through the snow for you, and there were those who wouldn't. Now, with nothing more serious than the Oscar show to prompt him, he simply needed a good listener who would first agree that it had been monstrous, then hear him out on some inconspicuous pluses he was beginning to see in the evening's events.

For one thing, it had served Pat as a healthy reminder that her illness was not the foremost thing in everybody's mind. It was impossible to draw that lesson from life around the house, where there was nothing but the helpful therapists and loving sympathy and more bouquets of store-bought flowers. But here was a stinging shot of reality for her, and one she wouldn't forget. People were going to slip up on her, including old friends.

More important, he was pleased with the strength of Pat's reaction. It was clearly the "appropriate emotional response" he had been warned was commonly lacking in stroke victims, and it held clues to the healing process going on inside her. It proved how very alert she was. She could follow everything said on a television broadcast. She had not looked questioningly to Angela or himself—she knew what she had seen and heard and she trusted herself to interpret it. She saw the lapse in manners, made all the right connections, perhaps even recalled times she had spent with Audrey five years before, when they were making *Breakfast at Tiffany's* together in New York. It was all very unfortunate; but there were some pluses, no denying it. In the end, Roald decided, the experience might even act as a spur to Pat's ambition.

Having made his calls, Roald settled down to a few hours' work. He seldom worked in the evening, certainly not if he had had a drink before supper. To him, the ideal for a writer was a session from ten to twelve in the morning and another from three to six in the afternoon, two good stints with a solid break in between, and the day's work laid aside by nightfall. That way you were always at your best—in fact, there was no other way to do it. But just now his days were so crowded with chores and concerns that there was no time for writing, and he was eager to get on with an account of Pat's illness which he had contracted to write for the *Ladies' Home Journal.*

There was no mystery about why he had taken on the *Journal* assignment. He needed the money. Pat's therapists alone were costing forty dollars a day, and this was coming after the loss of her salary for the film and a bad setback Roald had had with a movie script. Altogether, they were out something over a hundred thousand dollars. The Screen Actors Guild had paid most of Pat's hospital bills, and Martin Ritt, whose house they were renting, had written the day after the stroke to say that it was theirs, free, as long as they wanted to use it. Friends in New York had even taken up an impromptu collection. Still, the loss of so much income made every expense seem threatening. Here in California they were running through two thousand dollars a month or more, and Roald was worried that they might exhaust all their savings before they got back to England. The *Journal* piece would at least see them home—after that, if worst came to worst, they could sell some paintings.

Roald went to work on the article, having never before written anything like it and feeling vaguely embarrassed to be contributing to his own family's folklore. Once into it, though, he was grateful that he had it to do. He was tremendously proud of Pat, and writing about her was the best way he had to let others know. His love for her had always excluded great testaments and protestations. He preferred to let his feelings speak for themselves in daily living, and if caught red-handed in some tender act, he would huff his way out of it, laughing and blushing and denying it all. He had never kissed her in public, not even with words, and now it was so much easier for him to write of her strength and bravery than praise her to her face.

He also wanted to add a touch of humor to the dismal picture that had emerged of the family in the press. There was nothing tragic about them. They weren't cursed or doomed, and he despised having people approach him on tiptoe as if they were. The fact was that Pat was sublimely comic and clownish a great part of the time. Angela called her "a hoot," and even the real handkerchief-sniffers who came by to visit couldn't keep from laughing at some of the things she said. Fantastic words gushed out of her to replace those she had lost, wonderfully inventive new words, better and funnier than the ones she wanted. With the *Journal* piece to write, Roald had had an excuse to take notes:

> Sitting around kitchen at night, having a drink and smoking. Pat says: "Listen. Somebody . . . get me . . . a . . . sooty swatch."
>
> "A what?"
>
> "Oh, oh . . . you know . . . a . . . a . . . soapdriver."
>
> "A big soapdriver or a small one?"
>
> "Come on! Come on! You know what."
>
> "What?"
>
> "A . . . a . . . red hair drier."
>
> "You want a drink—is that it? A martini?"
>
> "That's it! A martini!"
>
> And again:
>
> "You give me the sinkers," she says, depressed.
>
> "You make me skitch."
>
> And later:
>
> "I want . . . a . . . a . . . I want an . . . oblogon."

"Somebody get Pat an oblogon."

"Stop it! I don't mean an oblogon. I mean a . . . a . . . a crooked steeple. God! You know!"

"A cigarette?"

"Ah! I love you! A cigarette. A cigarette. A . . . what did you call it? What word did you say?"

"Cigarette."

"Yes, cigarette. I'll go crazy if I don't have one. I'll jake my dioddles."

Sometimes they would laugh like fools while Pat's glare melted into an exasperated grin that finally gave way to her own true smile—her celebrated wide-screen smile, or the closest thing to it she could manage. She was a good sport, all right, and the teasing seemed to do her good, putting her at ease with herself and reminding her that certain touchstones of normalcy remained firmly fixed in place: Roald, as always, was getting after her.

Pat's good humor was crucial to Roald. He had made up his mind that a full recovery was possible as long as her morale held out. Depression was the only thing that could hold her back, and if that could be conquered, then all else could be too. He realized that his grounds for this belief were not entirely scientific. There was no conclusive way of telling how much permanent brain damage there might be and how much of what now appeared to be Pat's "deficits" would lighten and pass away in the course of the coming months. The speech therapist and the physiotherapist were equally guarded in their predictions, but they were getting obvious results.

Roald told Pat frankly everything she wanted to know, often supplying the questions as well when he sensed something troubling her. "Is it your leg you're worried about? Do you want to know what they say about your leg?" Sometimes he went well beyond mere factuality, as when he recounted all the details of her operation. But to the question of her ultimate chances, there was just one permissible answer—"one hundred percent," with no hedges or conditions.

Roald was aware that most doctors would have told him that total recovery was highly unlikely and that it was a risky business to build Pat's hopes too high. But he reasoned that if Pat was going to have to settle for some lifelong disability, she would be far better able to adjust to it after rebuilding herself as far as she could than she was now, all but helpless, just beginning. Shielding her from the hard probabilities of her future also allowed him to drive them from his own mind. He could not bear to indulge his own pessimism; it brought on a kind of paralysis deep inside his chest. He knew the feeling well, and he dreaded it.

The household remained defiantly cheerful, and Pat made it easy for the others. They basked in her smile as though it were a benediction, as indeed it was. Only some deep moral resource could account for such high spirits in the face of such an array of pains and bewilderments. When the smile came, its value was lost on no one. It became hard not to think of Pat as a person of saintly goodness when one considered how deeply she suffered in the silence of her smile. A universe lay shattered just behind her eyes, and it made one gulp with wondering admiration to sense for an instant the strength she was expending just to be friendly and gay.

Jean came from the hospital almost every day and would leave fairly floating on the joy Pat radiated to her. Jean shared a special sense of complicity with Pat. She had seen Pat at her worst, and Pat felt no obligation to perk up for her. Pat's visitors often left her tired and frustrated, and she would turn to Jean when they left and say, "Damn, damn, damn," shaking her fist at their departing backs. Jean remarked to Roald on the change that came over Pat when visitors were there; it was as if Pat's loneliness increased in proportion to the number of people in the room. Roald agreed—they mustn't overdo it.

Jean was not the only one who felt that Pat was especially relaxed when she was around. Anne Bancroft had the same impression. Anne was one of Pat's closest friends in the theater, but she was also Pat's most obvious rival. They were both actresses of the same general range, admired by the same audience, and they were also close in age and appearance—"weathered beauties," as Roald called them. Anne and Pat had each been given roles the other wanted, and could have played; Anne had won an Oscar for her role in *The Miracle Worker* the year before Pat won hers for *Hud*. But now Anne had replaced Pat in *Seven Women,* and it was evident that she felt uneasy about it.

Anne came by the house very often, volunteering any help she could offer. Anne knew far better than most when to talk incessantly and when to hold back and give Pat a chance to try to speak a few words. Many visitors seemed at their wit's end after five minutes with Pat, for it required some intuition to perceive whether Pat's lagging end of the conversation was due to speechlessness or simple-mindedness. Some guessed speechlessness and talked nonstop the whole time they were there; others assumed that Pat had been stricken back to childhood and addressed her in a kind of tragic baby talk that made even gentle Angela feel ill.

Pat herself was very restrained in showing her rage and confusion. Even when her intelligence was insulted with pidgin English ("Me make you cof-fee?"), she smiled on indulgently or laughed by way of subtle warning that there was a bit more to her than might meet the eye. She rarely attempted to speak when there was more than one person in the room with her. Listening to two people was like watching a tennis match played with a disappearing ball, and sitting in a roomful of chattering guests was an experience to compare with falling repeatedly from a speeding train. Words shot past like tracer bullets, laughter bubbled and burst inexplicably. Suddenly a word would arrive in all its tangle of meaning and implication, and for a second she would understand exactly what they were saying. But before she could focus her thoughts, before she could trap a word of her own, the thread would snap and her half-formed ideas would flee, unrecognized.

Not that this was always a torture. At times Pat felt almost serene, protected by her silence, free to drop out, amazed and admiring in the presence of her quick and clever friends. She couldn't get over how intelligent everyone had become—and Roald was an absolute genius. So she would sit forward in her chair, left leg crossed over right, forearms balanced on the knee, the left brown oxford tapping in the air, the right, with its ascending silver stirrup, planted heavily beneath her; she would sit forward and show signs of listening, knowing neither the names of her visitors nor what they were saying, her mind roving elsewhere or simply spinning free, the double vision in her eyes adding to her sense of drifting. And yet the eloquence of her smile and gaze made Jean and Anne and many others think that Pat had told them something that no one else could know.

The children were more elusive targets, and Pat's failures with them were the only disappointments that seemed to bother her. But even-tempered Theo often turned up to fill the space left by the others. He was Pat's great inspiration, and her eyes would shine at the very sight of him. She had seen him blind and drowsy and failing so often that the ebullient child dancing with excitement not a foot away from her was undeniable proof of the brain's magic gift for recovery. Theo's brain, like Pat's, held a mystery that only the passage of time would reveal; at his age, it was impossible to tell how much permanent damage had been done. It was barely a year since his hydrocephalus had been arrested, but Roald was optimistic. Theo made it hard not to suppose that everything would be all right. He was a great optimist himself, a fantastic little personality.

Theo was not perplexed by Pat's wordlessness. On the contrary, he appreciated it as a rare chance to do all the talking. He began every speech with a burst of starting syllables that made him twist with impatience, waiting for the first full word to come, but once he got started, he could have entertained on television. His range was as impressive as the speed of his delivery: budgerigars, sunsets, how to choose a necktie, the ABC's. Pat could not always follow him, but like everyone else she enjoyed trying.

Theo was ecstatic when he discovered that Pat was also a

student of the alphabet. The effects of her stroke interfered with every means of expression, and her speech therapist was teaching her to read and write, as well as speak. When Theo overheard them working together on the ABC's, he burned to join the class. As soon as the speech therapist drove away, Theo appeared with his collection of giant-size flash cards and began checking Pat out on the words he knew—SISTER, CAKE, ORANGE, TROUSERS. "Aaah-aaah!" he would say when she didn't know the word, pointing a finger and rolling his eyes shame-shame.

Roald let Theo run on with his games and quizzes, even when Pat tired and could not keep up the pace. The speech therapist had warned him that an hour or so of intense intellectual effort was all that Pat was up to in a day—after that, it was self-defeating, perhaps even harmful. But it seemed to Roald that idleness was far more dangerous than fatigue. The sight of Pat sitting vacant in a chair appalled him—to be empty, vegetating, anything was better than that.

Pat went to bed gratefully and was elaborately languid getting up. Whenever she could get away with it, she spent a tranquil hour drinking a cup of coffee, stretching it out, savoring it, appraising every sip. It wasn't that she was unwilling to go along with the cure; she believed Roald implicitly when he told her that hard work alone could save her. But from her first waking moment until the lights went out at night, every movement she made ran sharply against the grain of her inclinations. She was too short on volition to insist much on anything, but her instincts told her that the best thing she could do for herself was to curl up and rest, giving her wounds a chance to heal. Still, she let Roald run her, and that meant making each day a grueling exercise in denying her body all that it wanted.

The speech therapy sessions were almost a pleasure—no different, really, than Theo's games. She couldn't participate as she would have liked. Part of her mind remained disengaged, shocked and bewildered at the extent of its loss. But another part, the dominant part, grasped for the simple straws held out to her, the names of things, the alphabet, numbers, words. "My mind is gone" was among the first sentences she spoke, and she said it almost triumphantly: it was a sentence, after all. Everything she learned in these sessions turned out to be something she already knew, something hidden and now rediscovered—"Yes! Yes!" she knew these things. There was tremendous pleasure in this simple work. Her progress was swift enough to hold her excitement, and after the first few lessons she waited by the window for her teacher to come, searching the street for his car.

Physiotherapy was much less like a game and more like running through neck-high water. The exercises were boring and repetitive and there were no dramatic conquests. The muscles in the right leg and arm were slowly rebuilding themselves, and her hand was slightly more limber. Pat knew that this was work she had to do, but she did not wait by the window for it to begin.

The house purred along smoothly, even with all the visitors. Angela worked so hard in the kitchen that she began to worry about her health, but Roald didn't take that very seriously. Sarah was thriving on Ophelia's total dependence, and the maternal surge that rose up in her, making her cheeks blaze and her bosom swell, carried over to Tessa and Theo in pampering ways. That left only Pat and himself;

one absorbed in the process of recovery, the other in its management and technique. Considering how things had stood a month before, Roald felt no qualms at all about coloring his article an optimistic pink and sending it off to the *Journal.*

3

ROALD woke on the morning of their departure for home with a satisfying sense of order and calm. Had he been the sort to luxuriate in bed, this would have been the perfect occasion to lie there for a good half-hour, running through his well-laid plans for the day ahead. But he was up and dressed as quickly as ever, and it wasn't until he caught himself playing razor golf that he realized what a splendid mood he was in.

Razor golf had been a real compulsion with him years before. He couldn't shave without trying to reduce the number of strokes it took to get around his face. Even after perfecting a smooth jawbone drive that carried him from sideburn to sideburn in a single stroke, he had managed to break twenty only a half-dozen times. His long neck and angular features presented him with what he felt sure was an exceptionally challenging course. It was the upper lip that did one in—that, and the point of the chin.

Thinking about the game and the days when he used to play it caused Roald to lose count of the score, and he finished the shave with a flurry of short, noncompetitive strokes. He was not one to linger over tonsorial matters, and on his way back through the bedroom he brushed his thinning hair without bothering to consult a mirror. It was not yet eight o'clock, and Pat was still asleep. He closed the door softly behind him and went downstairs for coffee and a look at the paper.

Tessa and Theo were already at the breakfast table and Sarah was feeding Ophelia her morning mush. A wave of gratitude passed over Roald at the sight of them—how lucky he was to have found Sarah, this capable, sensible girl. It had not exactly been a question of luck, of course; the choice of a children's nurse was far too vital to trust to luck. Instead, he had conducted a talent search, beginning with detailed advertisements in the morning and evening papers of Glasgow and Dundee. After sifting through the fifty-odd replies and writing letters to the dozen or so who seemed to be likely candidates, he flew up to Scotland and interviewed each girl in her own home, thereby getting a glimpse of the kind of household she came from. He made a point of calling on them as early in the morning as possible to see if they were dawdlers, and indeed, all except three were still in bed when he arrived. Those three became his finalists, and all were flown down to spend a weekend at Gipsy House, the Dahls' home in Great Missenden. Sarah was everyone's first choice, a strong, plain girl, cheerful and intelligent. A police sergeant's daughter. The trouble he'd taken had paid off handsomely, as was evident in this morning tableau of healthy, well-fed children. The day was beginning without the merest ripple.

Most of the luggage was already at the airport, and the airline had promised two limousines in time to take them to a press conference Roald had set up for Pat. This was to be her first public appearance since the stroke, and it was important that it should go well for her. In some respects it was a bothersome extra in a day that was already too busy, but it would leave a poor impression if he were to spirit Pat off to England without a word to the press. People would conclude that she was incapable of answering a few simple questions. So he had called the local papers and the wire services and set up a meeting at the airport, asking only that they keep their questions clear and direct and that they not come out to the house to cover the departure. Pat was greatly excited at the prospect of talking to reporters again, and they had rehearsed together several times, with Roald playing the man from the *Hollywood Reporter*.

"Do you hope to make another film someday, Miss Neal?"

"Yes—yes, I do."

"When may we hope to see you in Los Angeles again?"

"In a year. I have a baby—I'm going to have a baby. That first, then I'll do it. Is that right? Oh, Papa, what do I say?"

Roald was sure she would pull it off nicely.

Pat looked lovely when she came downstairs. She wore a maternity dress with a candy-striped collar and a graceful satin coat that fell to the top of the brace. Her turban looked equally chic, and the eye patch, as part of the ensemble, had positive flair—a note of mystery, an incongruous devilish presence on the gay face Pat wore that morning. The only sure clue to her condition was the leg brace, and not so much the brace itself as the shoe from which it sprouted. The orthopedic oxfords, the nonskid invalid boots, the police matron specials. The shoes embarrassed Pat, but Roald defended them to the point of insisting that they were the one genuine fringe benefit of her illness. "What do you mean, 'they're ugly'? Why, I've been trying to get you into this type of shoe for nine years. My sister wears the very same thing. When people see you in these practical, good-looking shoes, they'll know what an intelligent woman you are."

The conference room at the airport was abuzz with reporters and cameramen when the family arrived. Pat walked in unaided and the newsmen rose and gave her a spirited round of applause. Roald answered a few preliminary questions—they would spend a few days in Washington visiting friends before proceeding to England. Then all attention turned to Pat.

"How are you feeling, Pat?" a reporter called out.

"I feel fine." The words were drawn out, pronounced slowly and with meaning.

"When do you think you'll be back to make a picture?"

"I'll be back to work in a year. The baby first! Then, one year, I'm sure."

"What have the doctors told you about the baby?"

"The prediction is . . . the baby will be . . . fine."

Prediction! Roald was amazed to hear the word dropped so smoothly into the sentence. Pat hadn't been dealing in words of such caliber since the stroke. And, in fact, that *was* the prediction, unsettling though it was to wonder how much it deserved to be believed. Pat's abdomen had been shielded with a lead apron during the long x-ray session on the night of the stroke, but one still sensed the danger inherent in subjecting a pregnant woman to so much radiation. It made Roald nervous to think about it, but the question had not shaken Pat's composure in the slightest. Evidently, Roald thought, she trusts what she's been told.

The conference was over in ten minutes, ending with shouted good wishes from the reporters and a cocky wave from Pat. She walked on her own through the lobby leading to the departure ramp, and although her limp was heavy and awkward, she seemed stronger than anyone had known she was, as though her voyage into the public eye had bolstered and encouraged her. There were more greetings, more waves, more kisses blown, and then they were on the plane, buckled in, rolling out on the runway. It was May 17, three months to the day since the stroke. Pat was enthralled when Roald pointed out the coincidence.

They had a good and happy time in Washington. Friends treated them like royalty, and Ethel Kennedy invited them out to Hickory Hill, where they spent a sunny afternoon chatting with various Kennedys while Tessa and Theo marveled at the menagerie of friendly animals and played with the troop of children. Everyone was careful not to exhaust Pat, but there didn't seem to be a chance of that. She was brighter and more talkative than she had been at any time in California, even in the company of people she hadn't met before. When they left on the night flight to England two days later, Pat was almost dizzy with excitement. She had a cigarette and a martini when the seat-belt sign went off, then slept without waking nearly all the way across. Roald took a sleeping pill, but it was deep into the flight across the ocean before he finally slept.

Roald's three sisters and their families were waiting at the London airport to welcome Pat home. Asta, the youngest, was the first to be spotted in the crowd; at an even six feet, she stood inches taller than any of the others. And there was Else with her beautiful twins, Anna and Louise. And Alfhild, the eldest sister, with Astri, her daughter. They beamed and waved across the customs barrier, and then they were together, a hearty circle of bear-hugging blond in-laws in the heart of the airport crush. Pat found herself crying, and she could not stop, could not account for her tears, could only smile through heaves of sobbing and try to tell them all that she hadn't cried like this since the illness began. The sisters did their best to conceal their shock at seeing Pat; they knew how ill she had been, but they hadn't imagined that she would look so punished and drawn.

They drove the twenty-five miles to Great Missenden in three separate cars, losing one another on the cloverleaves just beyond the airport, but all traveling the same accustomed route, through the gray industrial streets to the London–Oxford Motorway, which they followed until the turnoff brought them into the meadows and tree stands that spoke to them of their home. Buckinghamshire, the countryside green-on-green in the springtime, the fields broken by clumps of beech and juniper and by hedgerows exploding with bursts of hawthorn pink and red. Even the air seemed to have a substance lacking in America, a rich scent of loam and mowed grass, and the travelers drank it in for all that it meant to them. Roald felt genuinely moved at the sight of the land. It was only in springtime, coming home from America as they had so many times, that he realized how completely the country possessed him. He was a countryman, all right, and by the time they reached Great Missenden, his thoughts were turned wholly to his garden. The roses, the lilies, the clematis. The clematis would have spread across the garage wall.

They turned up the lane to Gipsy House and in another minute they were home. The lawn and the orchard looked lush and deep, and the first of the roses were already in bloom. But the moment they saw the front door, their hearts sank; it was a brand-new factory-smooth door. Good God, the decorators! Suddenly Roald remembered that some decorators had been working on the house while they were gone. He noticed that the old, worn nineteenth-century tiles in the doorway had been torn up and replaced with shiny new ceramic tiles. A chill settled over him as he led Pat inside, treading distastefully on the ghastly modern tiles.

It was worse than he could have imagined. The living room was painted chocolate-brown. Absurd curtains were everywhere. The kitchen seemed to have been flown in from California. Roald was numb. The sisters mumbled that they knew the decorators were getting out of hand but hadn't wanted to bother him, what with all his other troubles. After the full horror had sunk in, they began to notice the garden bouquets that blazed from the corners of every room. The kitchen table was stacked with homemade cakes and food, including a dozen brown eggs, some perfume spray and a bottle of champagne sent up by Mr. Thurgar, the village druggist. Roald cheered up at the sight of these gifts and proposed a toast to the pleasure of being home. At the first sip, Pat blinked in amazement and said, "It's gone!"

"What's gone?"

"The double eyes."

And it was true. Her eyes had slipped back into focus. The double vision had vanished, and that was the last of that.

4

IT WAS RAINING, it had rained every day for a week, and the roses and lilies were rotting on their stems. Theo's red wagon stood brimful of rain water and floating petals on the black flagstone terrace in front of the house. The lawn had become a deep and spongy moat that enclosed the house in a rich scent of country loam. Lights burned in every downstairs room, and Gipsy House, with its steam-free double windows, looked as clear and bright as an aquarium against the dark summer afternoon.

Pat and I were playing dominoes, or at least a game we played with dominoes—too simple, it seemed, to be the real thing. We had been playing for nearly an hour, and Pat's nest of dominoes was surrounded by her coffee cup, cigarette box, ashtray and matches, plus a scattering of score sheets torn from a stack of new memo pads. These were a gift to Roald from a friend in New York, and each had its own joke printed across the top: "FROM THE BATHTUB OF ROALD DAHL"; "FROM THE WINE CELLAR OF ROALD DAHL." Pat's large, rough figures crowded the pages with columns that looked like a child's sums.

Pat had a strong killer instinct for parlor games. She played with great secrecy and excitement, guarding her pieces from my eyes and rewarding herself with a loud cheer whenever she found the domino whose pips matched the last entry in the winding wall we had built across the table. Only her fingers failed her, and she left it to me to place her pieces flush and square with the others.

Pat's concentration went unbroken until Sarah appeared with a tray. "That's good! Very good of you!" Pat said, sweeping the dominoes aside in mid-game to make room for the tray; the game was instantly forgotten. "I love coffee . . . *so* much," Pat said earnestly. "That and cigarettes. I *love* cigarettes. When people are around me very long, they . . . quit."

"They quit smoking?"

"Yes, they quit smoking. They really do."

"Why?"

"They can't stand it."

"Can't stand seeing you smoke so much?"

"No, they can't. They quit because they can't."

"You horrify them."

"Yes."

"Your example frightens them."

"That's right. So they quit."

I laughed, but Pat was serious. She turned to look out the window.

We sat in silence at the round oak table in the living room. Tessa and Theo were watching a figure-skating show on the television set in the nursery, and alpine waltzes floated heavily through the house. In the kitchen Sarah and Jenny, the new cook, cackled over Don-mini—at fourteen months, Don-mini was learning to talk. Pat stared out the window at the rain-soaked garden, her coffee now forgotten. Pat's coffee mug, the souvenir of a film with John Wayne (To Pat Love DUKE—*In Harm's Way*), rested precariously close to her elbow. I reached over and pushed it away, not wanting to break her spell.

I had been sent to Gipsy House to interview Pat and Roald for *Life* magazine shortly after their return, but in almost a month of afternoons with Pat, I had rarely seen her still for so long a moment. When we weren't playing a game or running through a quiz, Pat's empty-handedness made her fidgety and nervous. She would lift herself out of the chair to go off on some imagined errand, then return a few minutes later in a new state of mind that canceled whatever conversation we had been having. When she saw that I was taking notes she would sit up brightly and smile, or demand to see what I had written, giggling eventually in her struggle to maintain a nice light atmosphere. I was impressed by the way she forced herself to appear in good spirits, even though her cheerfulness seemed incongruous and unwarranted much of the time.

Her efforts to show a happy face did not change the melancholy arc of her shoulders, nor her way of sitting in a chair. A chair seemed to wrap her in its arms, deflate her, sap her strength away. Standing or walking, she could be almost jaunty—sublimely pregnant, tall and commanding. She moved across a room like a sailboat tacking, touching down on tabletops and window sills, guiding herself through doors. But once she settled again, her lassitude would return, as though something deep within her were resigned to endless waiting.

"What month are we in?" Pat asked, turning back to the table.

"You're not going to believe this, Pat, but it's July," I said.

"That means I'm going to birth this baby next month."

"Right. What month will that be?"

"Next month will be . . . will it be August?"

"Right. And the next?"

"August, September, October, December—"

"You forgot November."

"November! God! Let me start with January. January, February, March . . ."

She ran through the months several times, faltering repeatedly at April and November, finally getting it right.

"And the names of the children?" I asked.

"The children are Tessa and . . . ohhhh, Theo. Tessa and Theo and . . . Don-mini. But Ophelia is her real name."

"And my name?"

"You're . . . Barry. Is that right? Barry?"

"Yes."

I felt uneasy about quizzing Pat. I was afraid to offend her by asking obvious, easy questions. But it was difficult to know where she lacked only words and where the concept behind them was missing. Her speech was slightly blurred, but easy enough to understand, and she usually seemed certain what she wanted to say even when she couldn't find the words, like a person struggling with a foreign language. But sometimes the meaning of her words fogged over as she spoke them, and although her tongue worked well enough, she made no sense at all.

"So tell me the story of your life," I said. This was another game, one that I preferred. I loved to hear Pat's stories, and encouraging her to tell them seemed a constructive way to work on both her memory and her speech.

"Where do I start?" Pat was eager to go.

"I was born in a small mining town in the West . . ."

"All right, all right. I was birthed in Packard—Packard, Kentucky. It was a town where they . . . dug for coal."

"A coal-mining town."

"A coal-mining town, but it isn't there any more. There was a dirt road, the only road in town. I remember my father's office, and my grandfather was the doctor. It was very small, mind you, and now it's gone. We moved to Knoxville when I was three. That was because my father got a better job. He was a bookkeeper in Packard, but then in Knoxville they made him a manager. He was called 'Coot.' That wasn't his real name, though. His real name was . . . William, I think."

"That's right, Pat." I had read through Pat's scrapbooks for all the names.

"William, then, and . . . oh, my mother's name is like my aunt's. Aunt Ima, so it's Ima and . . . Eura! My mother's name is Eura. Let's see, then—we moved to Knoxville I said, and I went to school there and I belonged to a sort of club of people who liked to act. I wanted to be an actress. I remember a movie called *A Little Girl's Name in Lights,* or maybe not like that, exactly, but something about a girl who becomes . . . a great actress, and my father took me to see it, and afterward I told him that was like me.

"Then after school I went to Northwestern, except that the war was on and there weren't any men there. We did plays, but there were no men in them. We took the men's parts, we girls. And then my father died after my first year at school. He died of a . . . you know, a . . . heart trouble, a heart attack. It was caused by being so fat. Gosh, he was fat. He weighed . . . *so much!* He tried and he tried, but he couldn't lose weight. Mother was skinny. And Pete and Margaret-Ann are skinny too. All of us kids were skinny.

"Anyway—what one thing were we talking about?"

"Your father died . . ."

"Yes, and it seemed strange going back to school after Daddy died. My Aunt Maude sent me for one more year, but I felt strange taking money, with Daddy gone and a little brother still at home. I was in a sorority and supposed to be having such a good time. It was Pi something—Pi . . . Phi? Yes, Pi Phi—it was that, my sorority. But the war was on and the school seemed like the wrong place to be. I went through that year, my second year, but then I wanted to go to . . . Broadway.

"So that next fall I got in a show, a traveling show, you know that goes around with a hit . . ."

"A touring company?"

"Yes, a road company, and the play was—oh, a famous play, a big hit, with a funny name . . . oh, I know it . . ."

"*The Voice of the Turtle.*"

"Yes, yes, that, and then I went to New York to live. And I got a job cutting pies in a big restaurant. I can't remember its name—I can't remember any names!—but it was a great big restaurant where you . . . went through the line. I was the one who came in at noon and, well, cut the pies."

Pat's amnesia could be selective, as though her memory faded where she wanted it to fade. It was not that she had trouble recalling moments of great trauma; Theo's accident and Olivia's death remained vividly present in her mind. She could also recall a wealth of vignettes from the distant past, anecdotes about people without names in which she still saw the humor or the moral. Sometimes a search for an identity would lead her into a Proustian recital of remembered facts that was astonishing for its acuity and richness of perception: "Oh, you know, that leading man, the one with the tiny, beautiful hands, and a voice that was just like them."

But she spoke of her career as if she were reciting the months of the year again; striving only to get the sequence right, she would tick off her movies and plays, one following the other in a mechanical shuffle of offers and contracts that had moved her back and forth across the country. The excitement of the life she had led seemed utterly absent from her memory of it.

Occasionally Pat could be persuaded to bring out her scrapbooks. They bulged with loose clippings and glossy marquee glamour shots. It was apparent that she had worked on them in brief spells up until five years or so before, when the last clippings had been pasted in. The batch of "profiles" and interviews done when she won her Oscar was crammed into a bundle with reviews of her most recent movies and wedged inside the cover of the last book she had started.

Pat's career could have been invented in Hollywood—as, indeed, a good share of it was. Her Broadway debut as the hateful Regina in *Another Part of the Forest* was among the most sensational ever. Just twenty years old, and with very little experience behind her, she won all the important awards as best Broadway actress of 1946. She was "the new Tallulah Bankhead," "clearly the actress we have long awaited," "the lovely new queen-elect of the American stage." Warner Brothers signed her to a long movie contract during the run of her play, and she left for Hollywood without doing another. "The new Garbo," Jack Warner kept saying in the clippings she had saved.

"I had such great—oh, what are they called? When you sign, you know, and they give money . . ." Pat had been running along fluently, and now she was exasperated at the want of a word.

"Do you mean contracts?"

"Contracts! I had bee-*yootee*-ful contracts. There was something in me that wanted to be a big star. A movie star. And, gosh, how they wanted me! It was very glamorous getting used to it. The first year I was there I had a . . . fur, a fox fur. I've still got it. It's upstairs in the closet. Naïve? Oh, gosh, yes, I was. It's fine to be naïve, and if girls aren't naïve at twenty, who's naïve ever?"

Hollywood misunderstood Pat completely. She was cast in heavy romantic roles, silly little comedies, sophisticated, lacquered-beauty roles—everything that was wrong for her. She made thirteen films between 1948 and 1952, with dismal results for both Pat and her studio. Her first movie, *John Loves Mary*, with Ronald Reagan and Jack Carson, left the critics enraged. "Patricia Neal shows little to recommend her for further comedy roles," said Bosley Crowther in a *New*

York Times review that Pat had neatly clipped and mounted with the others. "Her looks are far from arresting, her manners are slightly gauche, and her way with a gag line is painful. She has a long way to go and a lot to learn." *Time,* in its way, liked her somewhat better: "The picture's chief blunder is the miscasting of Patricia Neal, an able young Broadway actress whose throaty, stagy intensity in this featherweight role suggests a tigress in a cat show."

Then came *The Fountainhead,* with Gary Cooper, a dubious bit of social philosophizing in its time but now established as a classic of camp; *The Hasty Heart,* with Richard Todd and Ronald Reagan ("Ill-at-ease throughout"—the *New York Times;* "Embarrassing"—*The New Yorker*); *Bright Leaf,* with Cooper and Lauren Bacall ("Miss Neal plays the female tormentor as though she were some sort of vagrant lunatic. Her eyes pop and gleam in crazy fashion, her face wreathes itself in idiotic grins and she drawls with a Southern accent that sounds like a dim-wit travesty,"—the *New York Times*). She played opposite Dennis Morgan in *Raton Pass,* Van Heflin in *Weekend with Father,* Tyrone Power in *Diplomatic Courier,* John Wayne in *Operation Pacific* ("Miss Neal does not help matters in the least"—the *New York Times*), even Victor Mature in *Something for the Birds.* It was a dreadful beginning, and Pat's contract was not renewed. But there were a couple of films that have merited occasional art-house revivals—*The Day the Earth Stood Still,* with Michael Rennie, and *The Breaking Point,* with John Garfield, in which Pat delivers one of the immortal lines in the history of American cinema; as Coast Guard bullets rip into Garfield's charter boat on a secret night run in from Cuba, she sighs and says, "I guess I should have swam back to port—or is it 'swum'?"

The only other thing the clippings revealed about those years was a love affair with Gary Cooper, which Pat broke off after three years. It was a high-level open secret, protected only by the gossip columnists' reverence for marriage, until the Coopers briefly separated in 1951. "THE GARY COOPERS PART; IS PATRICIA NEAL NEXT?" ran the headline in the next morning's paper, and from then on it was a festival of tongue clicking in the fan magazines and gossip pages.

But Pat made a strong impression of honesty and courage in the way she dealt with the press. Until then, Hollywood reporters had not bothered to get far beyond her pet peeves (cats, caviar and opportunists), and the fact that she slept in a nightgown, with the window open, and was always either "delighted" or "thrilled" to be cast in any film. But when they came around on the Cooper story, Pat emerged as a frank and sensible person: "Am I in love with him? Could be. But I'd be silly to go around advertising it, wouldn't I? After all, he's a married man. Where does that leave me?"

Now, as her recital brought her to the memory of those days, Pat warmed to the telling. It was as though friendships and romances were stored somewhere else in her memory, apart from movies and plays. Pat knew on her own inner authority that she was finished as an actress, regardless of what Roald said—or talked her into saying. Her career was a completed episode, and looking back on it with all its names and labels stripped away, she perceived it as spilt milk, calmly and without enthusiasm. The friends, though, were still friends, and no delusion could upset her love for them. Her best friends then were best friends now; nothing was missing but the names.

"I left Hollywood because I'd been in love and it had . . . not worked," Pat said, rocking forward on her elbows, eyes wide. "Do you know who it was I was in love with?" she asked. "Gary Coop*ah*—that's right. Anyway, I thought that if I went to New York I'd get my life back like it was. And it worked, because I met Papa—Roald!"

⚙

Roald was spending this rainy July afternoon in his writing hut, his "Wendy house," as Theo had named it, a white clapboard building the size of a gatekeeper's shack out on the edge of the orchard. The Wendy house was divided into two rooms, neither more than six feet wide. Roald kept files of his manuscripts and papers stored in two old wooden cabinets in the front room. On top of the files were two model planes with slender oak propellers and long arching wings covered in varnished silk. A foam-rubber exercise mat lay folded in a corner, and against the wall were several heavy barbell sets, the largest as broad as a milk-truck axle. The back room was for writing—a cluster of tables and files and cardboard boxes drawn close around a soft leather chair, forming a kind of cockpit, or cocoon.

Roald was not in the least eccentric in his approach to his work. When there was no emergency to divert him, nor all the household chores he now had to do, he went regularly, even punctually, to the Wendy house, working three hours in the morning and two in the afternoon, and returning to the house in much the same mood as when he left it. The ritual did not vary. Equipped with a thermos jug of hot coffee, he would stride the fifty paces from the house, light the Aladdin Blue Flame heater against the permanent chill of his hut, sharpen a half-dozen Dixon Ticonderogas to an accountant's taste and settle down in his chair, tucking his lap robe snugly around his legs, pulling the gooseneck lamp down to the level of his forehead, and finally sealing himself into position with his felt-covered writing board, an instrument of his own design which rested on the arms of the chair to form a smooth, wide tray with a form-fitting inside curve that touched his chest just below the heart. He did all his writing on legal-size yellow pads, filling the pages with his fine, spidery script, then going back to weed and hone with further indecipherable squiggles between the narrow lines. He was a slow and careful worker, but he suffered no blocks or dry spells and his concentration was steady and intense. If for any reason he was needed in the house, his lamp could be flashed from a switch in the nursery. One flash meant someone was asking for him and two meant an emergency; the only time the lights had flashed twice was the day Olivia died.

Given a clear stretch of time in which to work, Roald would run through an even gross of pencils in a year. A year, a good year, might produce three short stories—twenty or thirty thousand words. A fourth collection of stories remained Roald's prime ambition, but that would take three or four years and required a solid sense of financial security before he could even begin thinking about it. And now, with the stroke, that was utterly gone. For Pat's sake it was important to insist that when she was completely recovered, she would be able to work again, but realistically, one couldn't count on it. And if Pat wasn't able to work, he would have to find something a good bit more profitable to write than short stories.

Roald had changed dramatically over the years—he knew it and was proud of the mental agility it displayed. At Repton, the prep school where he captained the squash and handball teams and also played football, he was passed through the grades with undistinguished marks, the classic young gentleman's beginning. Then, at twenty, Shell sent him off to Africa, a shining god of British commerce, or, as he later saw, a silly young man in charge of twenty Indian clerks.

He might well have gone carefully up the corporate ladder, becoming area supervisor, foreign operations chief, sales manager, perhaps; the life seemed far from disagreeable. But then accident—two accidents—had intervened to change the course of his life. The first occurred in the RAF when a burst of machine-gun fire brought his Gladiator down in flames. He had enlisted when the war broke out, driving alone across a thousand miles of jungle road to join the training squadron at Nairobi in October 1939. He trained there, and at the British airfield on Lake Habbaniya in Iraq, before being assigned to a fighter squadron in Egypt, flying bi-wing Gladiators against the Italians in the Western Desert. In September 1940, less than a month after he had finished his training, his plane was hit by machine-gun fire while strafing a convoy of trucks south of Fûka, a village not far from Alexandria, and the flaming crash-landing he made earned him three months in the hospital and a much-altered life.

His face must have hit the reflector sight in front of the windshield, because all the damage was to the upper half; the skull was fractured, the nose bashed in, and both eyes stayed closed for ten days. Plastic surgery left him slightly better-looking than before, but the hit on the head must have joggled the brain fairly hard, for almost immediately he detected a change in himself. Before the accident he had been a moderately normal fellow, with no affinity for the arts or anything of the kind. Roald had been told that his father, believing firmly in the power of prenatal influence, had taken his wife for long, lovely walks, told her tender stories, showed her beautiful pictures—but the boy who was born to them was resoundingly average in all respects but size. After the accident, however, he began to take an interest in beautiful things.

No sooner was he out of the hospital than he was sent on to Greece to fly the new Hurricane in the first campaign against the Germans. He had what the Air Ministry called "a very busy time of it," in which all but four of the thirty planes in his squadron were lost. Roald scored four kills, but he was suffering increasingly from head and back aches resulting from his crash, and in June 1941 he was sent back to England on the disabled list. At a dinner party in London he met Harold Balfour, then Undersecretary of State for Air, and the next day he was called to Balfour's office and told that he was going to Washington as an assistant air attaché.

In Washington the second accident caused him to discover himself as a writer. The United States had just entered the war, and since Roald, as a veteran combat pilot, was a rare bird indeed in America, the *Saturday Evening*

Post sent the novelist C. S. Forester to do an article about him. They had such a pleasant lunch that Forester didn't get around to doing his interview. Roald volunteered to put a few notes together and mail them in.

Roald had always been conscious of having a certain flair for writing. His letters were praised throughout the family, and even at nine he had written an essay on an exploration to the South Pole that began with a paragraph he was still proud of:

"Ever and anon the Black Bottom plowed steadily through the foaming billows which played restlessly on the ship's bow. Soon an iceberg was sighted and another and then another, floating lazily about in the still ocean which was now and then disturbed by a whale rising to the surface."

But he had never considered making anything of the writing; his only notes on the war were laconic entries in his logbook:

> One JU 88 recco intercepted over Haifa. Walked away from me—but got in one good burst, rear gunner silenced. . . . No petrol to operate, much bombing all around. . . . Ground strafe Baalbeck, 3 Dewoitines destroyed. Several women being shown over bombers on ground got shock of their lives. Much machine-gun opposition.

He spent a day or two working up some notes for a story, and when Forester saw what he had written, he thought it so good that he sent it directly to his editors under Roald's name. The *Post* bought it immediately, published it without changing a word, and signed Roald up to write more like it. In his astonishment at being taken so seriously Roald worked very hard, and soon his by-line was appearing everywhere at once—the *Post, Tomorrow, Collier's, Harper's,* the *Ladies' Home Journal, Town & Country.*

Roald gladly made the most of his new life as a writer. Walt Disney bought the movie rights to his very first story, a juvenile about gremlins which he had written in 1943, and dolls were made and songs written about these imaginary creatures. ("Gremlin" was Roald's contribution to the dictionary, a word he had coined to name a race of aerial saboteurs during the war.) Eleanor Roosevelt became a fan and invited him to the White House and to Hyde Park for weekends. Bernard Baruch befriended him, and Mrs. Ogden Reid made him her house guest whenever he was in New York. His first book, a collection of the magazine stories entitled *Over to You,* was published in 1945. They had been written quite fast: ten stories in two years, all of them about fliers and flying in the RAF. Those were years when Roald was discovering himself as a writer, and although he would later stand by what he had written, what he had said about the war, the stories themselves seemed amateurish to him.

It was not until after the war, when he began building his second short-story collection, that Roald found his pace and style. He had returned to England in 1945, and moved into his mother's cottage in Deep Mill Lane, less than a mile from the house where she now lived. He thrived on the country quiet and wrote much of his best and most serious work there. Besides turning out short stories (which appeared in *The New Yorker* as soon as they were submitted and in 1953 came out as a collection of nineteen stories under the title *Someone Like You*), he also had a book published in 1948 called *Sometime Never.* The novel was a strangely convincing fantasy about gremlins, but it could not be called a very great success; the celebrated editor Maxwell Perkins had commissioned it, then died with the manuscript on his nightstand.

Apart from breeding and racing greyhounds, and finding time to cultivate his interest in wines, antiques and paintings, Roald had nothing to distract him from his work. His earnings were sufficient for him to pursue his quiet life, paying his mother a little for room and board, collecting a few small paintings, betting on the dogs, visiting New York every year or so. The tempo never varied, nor did the quality of his work. The short stories were all sculpted from large ideas, and their structure imposed a fine tension between humor and irony on the one hand and grinning-skull horror on the other, a tension kept alive by the texture of the language and the subtle, inevitable tone of the secret moralist; they were stories of truth and consequence. It was New York that welcomed him most warmly as a literary man, and in 1947 his friend Charles Marsh persuaded him to return. By 1952, when he and Pat met, he was living there most of the time, *The New Yorker*'s odd English writer, every season's bachelor-of-the-year.

After he and Pat were married the following year, they lived in New York, and her income from stage and television work made it possible for him to continue at his measured pace through six more years, which brought a third book of stories. With typical ironic relish, Roald called it *Kiss Kiss*. The book came out in 1960 and was met with reviews that secured Roald's reputation as a master storyteller. But having finished it, he began to look closely at the work of other short-story writers and was struck by how every one of them seemed to get worse and worse as he churned out the stories.

So he decided to attempt a children's book. He worked on it for six months, enjoying the novelty of the form without really knowing if it was going to be any good or not. But *James and the Giant Peach* received such a warm reception that Roald could not resist trying another.

The next book, *Charlie and the Chocolate Factory*, turned out to be a much more complex project. The original idea was based on Roald's own fascination with candy. At school he had had a housemaster who once a year passed around a box with new and different kinds of chocolate from a candy factory which the boys graded according to taste. Roald drew from these experimental tasting sessions a vision of the inner workings of great chocolate factories, where somewhere at the back of the plant scientists and chefs labored in the inventing room, mixing and baking until one of them would cry, "Taste this! I think I've hit it!" All his life Roald had remained a candy-store connoisseur, faithful to the chocolate bars of his childhood, yet always ready to sample anything new; he could name a hundred English candies, easily.

Charlie turned out to be an even greater success than *James,* at least among children. There appeared to be a cult of spinster librarians in the United States who suffered from a pathological abhorrence of anything the least bit violent in a book written for children, and the trade reviews contained any number that ended with their chilly kiss of death: *"Not recommended for libraries or schools."* But the letters that still arrived at the house in bundles several times a week proved to Roald the soundness of his theory that violence appeals to a child's sense of humor so long as you make it happen flat out. If you have to do away with someone in a children's book, then have his head off, crunch him up, run him over—and the children will roar with laughter. Incontestably the children's favorite passage in *James* is where the two old ladies are crushed by the peach, and in *Charlie,* the children liked the scenes in which the nasty characters have something terrible happen to them, as when Augustus Gloop falls into the chocolate stream and is sucked up the pipe to the fudge room.

The children's letters left Roald filled with delight. It was one thing to have a certain literary reputation as the reinventor of the Gothic tale, but it was something entirely different to be a classroom hero to readers who paid you back for your work with crayon drawings of your best scenes. And only a few mornings ago a letter had come from a girl in Ohio: "Will you please write a book now called 'Tura, George and Kathleen and the Ooompa-Loompas'? Send one to me and one to my teacher and keep one for yourself. Love, Tura." Surely such inspired urgings would not be unwelcome in any writer's mail.

The children's books gave a breadth to Roald's career that even another collection of stories couldn't have done, and he took unconcealed pleasure in his triumph. It was, moreover, a source of income as well as pride to have four books spanning ten years all in print and selling nicely, multiplying themselves amoebalike in translations and new editions and anthologized fragments that filled three shelves in the house—*Kiss Kiss* in French and Portuguese, *Someone Like You* in Japanese and Danish, so many handsome new German editions of everything that Roald was hard pressed to maintain his old hatred of the Hun.

After *Charlie,* Roald wrote another children's book, *The Magic Finger,* then his first original screenplay, for a film to be called *Oh Death Where Is Thy Sting-a-ling-a-ling?*, and a rather delicate and dangerous short story dealing with murder by fornication. *The Magic Finger,* which was written within the limits of some pedagogue's idea of an eight-year-old's vocabulary, did not live up to *Charlie* or *James,* and the movie, with Gregory Peck in the lead, was cashiered as unproduceable after six disastrous weeks of mayhem in the Swiss Alps, where the action was set. Only the short story could be considered a success, since it won *Playboy*'s Story of the Year award, giving Roald an honorary key to all the Bunny clubs.

Now Roald was unsure what his next step should be, but in any case, there was no time for writing at this time; there hadn't been for five months, not since February. Days had passed without an hour to spare away from the chores of the house, and even now that he had organized a team of neighbors to work with Pat, the time he had to himself was almost entirely consumed by the mail. He still had several hundred letters to answer before he could think about returning to work. It was an English trait perhaps, but to Roald a letter ranked with a visitor waiting in the hall, and he had always begun his days by dealing with his correspondence. Now there was a bit too much to allow a careful answer to every one, but the minimum was a post card, and Roald, who couldn't type and had never dictated to a secretary, attacked the job in the only way he knew, with coffee and comforter in the wendy house.

The letters were like a scrambled treatise on suffering and hope. Nearly all were addressed to Pat, and most had been sent in the first month of her illness, when her name was in the papers every day. Roald had already answered at least a thousand like them, but he still examined each one, especially those written by stroke patients themselves. The letters from relatives and friends were full of advice, some of it excellent, and taken together they amounted to something approaching the sum total of folk wisdom on the mysterious calamity they all shared. Considering the deplorable incomprehension one found at every turn in seeking medical advice, there was much of value in these witnesses' accounts, and there was also much that made Roald shudder at the bitterness and stupidity that plagued the lives of so many survivors; many letters left a very clear image of the silent victim doomed by a self-pitying husband or wife.

The stroke patients' letters were strangely fascinating. Their oddities were endless, and reading them was often a cryptographic challenge, not only for the various ways in which their language or handwriting faltered, but also for their patterned eccentricity, the logic that was to be discovered in the way they wrote and thought. Sometimes the letters were terribly poignant for the evidence of the writer's impairment in words meant to convey encouragement and pride: "I herd you are sik like me in this mornings papr. But I tell you Pat you can lik this so-called stroke. One year I count that I was like somebody dead. Now all is bettr and sonn now I will be working like befor." Many spoke of their loneliness and sense of isolation; it was clearly the dominant emotion expressed in all the mail. But the brave ones had an answer to it. "Don't sit alone," one man wrote. "Don't sleep in the day. Stay awake on your feet if you can. My stroke was six months ago, two days after yours."

Roald built a tidy stack of post cards and letters before his empty thermos informed him that it was time to quit. The rain, he saw, had become a fine drizzle, and the dispersing clouds promised rainbows before sunset. He crossed the garden to the house, regretting that the lawn was far too wet for a game of bowls. Through the window he could see Pat exhorting Sarah's unmoving silhouette. At a distance Pat's struggle to express herself gave her an appearance of great animation and oratorical flair, with a lavish, Italian use of the hands that coaxed understanding out of the air. Seeing that she was still happily occupied, Roald changed course, deciding to drive up to Olivia's grave, with a stop to visit his mother on the way.

Roald's mother, who had been a widow for forty-five years, spent the better part of every day reading through a magnifier in the glassed-in terrace that served her as hot house and solarium. Roald was four years old when his father died of pneumonia, and the only vivid recollection he had of him was how, after losing an arm, he complained of great difficulty slicing the tops off boiled eggs. His father had been a canny immigrant ship broker in Cardiff and had left the family a quarter of a million pounds. The money amply took care of their needs, but even so, it had been no small accomplishment to send all the children to the best schools in what to her, a genteel young lady from nineteenth-century Norway, was a brash foreign land. In the past ten years the children had watched infirmity steal over her with an almost imperceptible grace, dimming her sight and hearing, and forcing her into her chair. Since selling her electric wheelchair to the Dame of Sark some years before, she had been strictly an indoors person. She was a large and very heavy woman, and in old age she had acquired a regal presence that fully compared to her queenly name: Sophia Magdalena Hesselberg Dahl.

Mumu, or, more strictly, Mormor, the Norwegian appellation by which this imposing matriarch was called, lived with Mrs. Newland, her housekeeper and companion, in a wing of John and Else's house. Else was the most solicitous of her children, and John the most manageable of her sons-in-law; and eighteen-year-old Nicky and the twins were there to reward her with the pleasure of watching bright and beautiful grandchildren growing up around her. Across the wide garden in back of her solarium she could just make out a corner of the amazing three-story tree house, where Nicky was spending the summer in artistic isolation from his family. And by living at Whitefields, as the house was called, Mumu was still no more than an hour's drive away from her other three children. Gipsy House was an easy five-minute drive, and Roald made it very often.

He arrived at the house to find his mother in an entertaining mood. She was feeling some pride in her psychic powers, and she wanted to impress Roald with the details. She had predicted Pat's recovery the day after the stroke, citing a dream in which she had attended a service for Pat wearing brown shoes; hence it could not have been a funeral. Now her soundings told her that Pat's baby would be a girl. Another girl would complete for Roald a family exactly like her own: two girls, a boy, then two more girls. And in both cases the eldest child had died before the age of eight, died in the month of November.

Roald held back from being openly credulous, but he did grant his mother some kind of crystal vision. Very often she had amazed them all by such feats as announcing the arrival of some unexpected visitor an hour in advance. She felt doom and catastrophe coming on from a great distance, sensing it and suffering it long before it happened. Her spiritualism was a matter of hypersensitivity—not always welcome, a kind of curse, in fact—and it drew nothing from occult science. But when Roald had told her that for a while after Olivia's death he was tempted to invite a celebrated male witch from Oxfordshire to have a go at exorcising possible evil forces from Gipsy House, it was clear from Mumu's enthralled response that she was sorry it hadn't been done.

Roald plucked sickly leaves from a shelf of coleuses while he listened to her talk. The solarium held more plants than she could cope with herself, and Mrs. Newland, who was completely reliable in all other departments of practical nursing and housewifery, did not always notice the odd albino stem that meant that a leaf was about to drop. He stayed with his mother for another ten minutes, then started out for the cemetery.

The graveyard was in Little Missenden, another mile and a half beyond Whitefields, over pasture land dotted with clumps of new houses. The village was smaller and finer than Great Missenden, and its softly looping main thoroughfare was seldom bothered by passing trucks or cars. The street was lined with a number of good sixteenth- and seventeenth-century houses, and a church, the Dahls' church, whose Norman font had stood secure for more than a thousand years. The graveyard was across the road from the church, and Olivia's grave lay in the back, fifty paces from the wooden gate.

It was a wide grave, a double plot, unmarked by any stone. Almost by reflex they had ordered one soon after Olivia's death, and Pat had chosen what seemed like a beautiful inscription: SHE STANDS BEFORE ME AS A LIVING CHILD. But when it arrived from the cutters they could hardly bear to look at it, and the headstone remained in the spot where they had banished it three years before, at the back of the garage, face to the wall.

Instead, Roald had proposed building a rock garden that would replace the horror of a gravestone with a living shrine to Olivia, who loved animals and flowers and knew them all by name. He consulted the leading English expert on alpine miniatures for help in choosing the plants. He drove around to quarries throughout the district in search of the proper rocks, then hauled them in with several yards of special rock-garden soil and laid them with a mason's care in a mound of crags and slopes and valleys pocketed with earth. The horticulturist suggested a great many different plants—minuscule hybrids, Japanese dwarf evergreens, wild mountain flowers—and Roald selected nearly all of them. Together they set in the plants, nearly two hundred specimens, arranged in convincing relation, as in a woodland terrarium. Then Roald added a dozen small porcelain animals from Olivia's menagerie, placing each in a spot that fit its shape and scale. The job consumed him for more than a month, and when he was finished he had built a small mountain, a rare and affecting garden one could look at for hours. The only indication that it marked a grave was Olivia's name on a small metal tag, like those used for labeling flowers.

Roald was not pleased with the look of the grave in the evening light of this darkening day. The grass around it was shaggy and tufted, and the week's rain had leeched soil away from the plantings, making them look threatened and sparse. He simply hadn't had the time to give it the care it needed. He seldom visited the grave without putting to use the old lawnmower he kept hidden under a nearby tree; now he brushed the grass with his fingertips before reconciling himself to the obvious—it was far too wet to cut. He weeded around the grave and examined the plantings to make sure that none had lost its footing in the soil. The garden was in better shape than he had feared. Given a decent day or two, he told himself, he would have it looking fine again.

He crossed the road to the church. Tacked to the door was a handlettered notice signed by the Reverend Francis Roberts, vicar of the Church of St. John the Baptist. Roald stopped to read it and was startled to see that it announced the safe return home of Patricia Neal Dahl and reminded the parishioners to persist in their prayers for her recovery. It was some time since he had set foot inside the church, and with Pat settled into a mood of estrangement from God, it no doubt would be a good while yet before they resumed their place in the congregation.

Not that it had been a very central place. They had contributed some money and time to the restoration of the frescoes in the chapel, and as Francis himself liked to put it, they were on a Christian-name basis with the vicar. Before Olivia's death they had attended Sunday services only occasionally. But then Pat was taken by a surge of religious feeling as dramatic and categorical as its absence was for her now. In both spells Roald followed her lead, accompanying her to church while the need of it was with her, and just as happily staying home now that it was gone.

Religion in the formal sense was extraneous to Roald's beliefs, which he had never identified beyond sensing in himself a basic confidence in the survival of man. He admired the works of the church and the spirit of its people, but his own spirit found no particular solace or inspiration within the walls of churches. He considered himself to be an undemonstrative but still religious person, and the same, he thought, was true of Pat. Her spate of enthusiasm for the church was really no more characteristic of her than her flat rejection of it; both were means of adjusting to calamities, and one was probably as helpful as the other. Her faith stood renounced at the moment because so many beastly things had happened to her. And if God was as they said He was, these beastly things couldn't possibly have happened when she hadn't been beastly herself. The religious boys had a very weak argument against that, he reflected, pulling open the heavy oak door and entering the darkened church.

He went to the light panel and switched on all the lights in the chapel and nave. It was a beautiful church, with thirteenth-century windows and a wealth of wall paintings and frescoes, some of them dating from the early twelfth-century. Inside the chapel, there was a spot on the wall scarred by small irregular crosses, scratched there for luck by Early Christian soldiers on their way to the Crusades. High on the wall near the altar was an antique Spanish carving of St. Catherine that Pat and Roald had given to the church in Olivia's memory. It jutted out from the wall like the figurehead of an unseen ship. Roald looked up at it for a long moment. Then he placed a few pounds in the offering box, switched off the lights and went home.

• • •

Roald arrived just in time to make drinks for the assortment of sisters and nieces and nephews and friends who turned up every day at the cocktail hour as though summoned there by bells. Else and John, Alfhild and her daughter, Astri, Angela Kirwan in a damp white tennis costume, the timorous Marjorie Clipstone. The conversation of large groups still lost Pat, with its speed and randomness, leaving her the choice of either doing all the talking or else remaining silent. Tonight, it appeared, was a night to do all the talking. Everyone wore a look of interest and concern, and they greeted Roald with their eyes alone, not wanting to interrupt Pat.

". . . and I woke up not believing. I always believed before. I don't understand it. I just didn't believe any more when I woke up." It was getting to be a favorite theme with her, and Roald was faintly impatient to be hearing it again.

"That's because you expected to see a glorious vision and you didn't," he said.

"No, I didn't, that's right," said Pat.

"Well, you were just misled by Katherine Anne Porter and Willa Cather and some other rather hysterical novelists who exercise their writing skill by describing what they hope to God they'll see when they die."

"What? What did you say?" Pat asked.

"I said that no one can know what the dead know. We have no reason to believe that death comes with any theatrical side effects. There doesn't have to be a vision of God to prove that God exists."

Pat was stumped by this and did not attempt to answer. Marjorie, the family's closest friend in the village despite an anxious, hesitant manner that always made her seem to be present on some kind of probation, tried diluting Roald's words into a pablum that Pat could swallow: "What Roald means, I think, Pat, is that the fact that you survived is itself a kind of proof . . ."

But Roald was having none of it. "No, no," he said. "The point is that whatever visions we might have or hope to have don't mean anything about the nature of life or death. You can feel cheated if you like, but it won't do you any good if you're meant to die."

"So if you die, you just die, and then you're dead," Pat said reproachfully. "You don't see . . . anything."

"I don't know, Pat," said Roald. "You have to die to find that out."

Pat was again at an impasse. Was her brain working right? she wondered. She knew that if she had died during the coma she would have gone unprotesting and unblessed, with no awareness that her life was ending. Was she wrong to be worried about it? Was she wrong not to believe? Roald seemed to think so. And yet, if death was such an empty thing, what did that mean for Olivia? Her thoughts were trapped in a morbid circle that always spun back to Olivia.

The conversation had splintered into a babble of parts. Pat reached out and tapped me on the wrist. When I turned around, her earnest look made me draw closer.

"How long are you buried . . . before you . . . come apart?" she asked.

"What do you mean, Pat? In the grave?"

"Yes. How long are you in the grave before you're just a . . . you know, just bones."

"Just a few months, Pat," I said. "Inside of a year it's all over, no matter what kind of coffin or embalming."

Pat let out a moan that rose almost to a shriek. I was

stupefied and panicked. Everyone fell silent. "I'm sorry, Pat, I'm sorry," I said, but her distress was too deep to be so cheaply cured. Roald leaned over and asked me what had happened. "Ah, yes, she was wondering about Olivia," he said. I was appalled at my faux pas—how could I have not remembered Olivia? "Pat, Pat, forgive me, I'm sorry," I said, but I wasn't getting through.

"How about the tapes?" Roald asked brightly. "Did you make a tape for Betsy this afternoon?"

To my amazement and relief, Pat brightened immediately. "We did!" she said. "You all must hear it."

First they played the tape her old friend Betsy Drake had sent from California a few days before. Her farewell gift to Pat had been a small tape recorder that matched her own so that they could keep in touch without the need of letters. Betsy's tape seemed to have been made at a party. There was a swooshing noise in the background that sounded like the surf, and a constant tinkle that was definitely ice cubes, plus snatches of laughter and happy talk. Betsy spoke first and then came a parade of familiar voices:

"Hello, Pat, this is Betty Bacall from California . . ."

"Pat, this is Zsa Zsa. All my love, darling . . ."

Pat listened to the tape for the twentieth time with shining eyes and a wide smile.

Pat's reply lasted barely two minutes, but she had worked hard on it for well over an hour. The idea of recording her voice intimidated her at first, causing her to forget what she wanted to say. I would set the tape spinning and Pat would strain at the brink of a word until finally her hold would slip, sending her into helpless laughter. Then she would ask to hear the laughter played back, and that would make her laugh again. It wasn't until I prepared a sheaf of cue cards that she began to get into it, and then her poor reading sabotaged a dozen attempts. She wanted her tape to be perfect, with no hesitations or stumbles, and she started from the beginning time and time again before she managed to get through to the end in a single try. The sound of her recorded voice delighted her; as Roald threaded the tape through the recording gates and fixed it to the spindle, Pat grinned around the room with anticipation. Roald clicked it on.

"Hello, Betsy, my dear, dear friend," said the voice from the recorder. *"Everyone here is well and fine. I am working every day and getting much better. Everyone says I am amazing. I am dying to birth my baby but I still have to wait. Papa says it will be soon now but it seems a long time to me. Life is going to be like it was, so don't you worry, my friend. Everything's going to be all right, all right!"*

5

"WHAT are you going to name the baby, Papa?" Pat asked. Riding in the car did not really make her nervous, but she kept her eyes fixed squarely on the road ahead as she spoke. Roald drew long on his pipe before answering, steering with one hand at the safe, observant forty miles an hour that was his accustomed clip on the last leg home from Oxford.

"Oh, I don't know," he said. "I was rather thinking of Dwight."

"Dwight! Oh, come on. Really what?"

"Really. Dwight. Dwight D. Dahl—an American child for you."

"But that's . . . that's too . . . *ugly*."

"Then you must help me think of another. I warn you that I'm leaning strongly toward Dwight D. Dahl."

"Oh, you know I can't think of names. I can't think of

anybody's name." Her amnesia no longer engaged her; instead she had taken to announcing it many times a day, announcing it as a simple fact about herself: "I can't remember names."

They had gone to Oxford to see Pat's obstetrician, Dr. William Hawksworth—or, as they called him, The Hawk. Dr. Hawksworth was a silver-haired consultant, a doctor's doctor, a thoroughly professional man; for this birth, both Pat and Roald needed all the reassurance that his learned manner could convey. In addition to the sixty x-rays taken at the time of the stroke, there had been eleven hours of anaesthesia, a great many drugs and medicines, and then the coma itself, fourteen days with the body stiff and unmoving. Even under the best of circumstances, the odds had to be slightly longer for a thirty-nine-year-old woman having her fifth child; Roald had heard that the fifth was often tricky—why, he didn't know.

But The Hawk had calmed them with his rare brand of breezy, chuckling confidence, and after examining Pat, he had agreed to induce the birth two weeks early. This was a great psychological victory for Pat. At the time of the stroke, the child inside her gave her something crucial to live for, and it was not beyond imagining that even during the coma some profound maternal instinct had helped urge her back to life. But now, eight months along, the pregnancy was retarding her, making walking extremely difficult and tiring, causing her to lose all hope about her appearance, forcing her into inactivity and depression. "When *am* I going to have this baby?" had become less a question than a lament.

It upset Roald to see Pat's energy dwindle as radically as it had in the past few weeks. In California any number of well-intentioned people had told him that he could look forward to seeing her recovery nine-tenths complete inside six months—and now the six months was almost up. The explanation that came with this advice was that the brain tissue that had been merely "insulted" by the pressure of accumulating blood would return to its function within that space of time. The remainder of the damage, if any, could pretty well be counted as permanent. There would be swift and dramatic progress while the injured tissue restored itself, but after that, the rate of improvement would taper off sharply and they would then discover the new shape of their lives. The aim in telling him this was always to offer some encouragement, to make the suspense more endurable by outlining an end. Don't worry, they meant to say, in just six months you'll know where you stand.

Roald had never been attracted by this notion, and he had resisted setting any date for the end of the convalescence, even when Pat begged to know how long it would take. Since it was evident from Pat's very first words that there had been no damage to the speech center itself, he felt confident that she would not encounter any functional barriers in regaining the lost means of expression. Aphasia is no more than the loss of language, amnesia the loss of memory, and the technique of rehabilitation, he felt, was a process hardly different from educating a child. You couldn't say when it would be over; it was not something that ended, it was something that grew.

He also thought it simplistic to believe that the brain would respect any deadline in doing its magic work of restoration. The brain could literally re-create itself, transferring the authority for many lost functions to uninjured zones, even in the case of really massive damage. There were so many mysteries, so many subtle factors of health and morale, and the kind of mortal luck in which the fraction of a millimeter might decide the difference between recovery and hopeless impairment; with so many combinations of unknowns, it seemed to him audacious to think in terms of a timetable. A healthy brain, no matter how plain or sluggish, was quite properly considered a galaxy unto itself. An injured brain was nothing less majestic.

And yet here was Pat, drifting into a defeatist curve that was undoing all the hard work of rehabilitation. A slack look had come over her, a look of shameless, physical boredom. He could scarcely persuade her to brush her hair. Her attention span was half what it had been a month before, and she had lost all enthusiasm for her lessons, her exercises, even the children. She stayed in bed as late as she could in the morning, took a two-hour nap after lunch, and then at night was still so exhausted that she was often in bed before dark and asleep the instant her head touched the pillow. Her sleep was dreamless, heavy, surrendering; when the children cried out in the night she did not wake up.

Only in games and at the cocktail hour would a hint of her spirit return. She was always happy to see visitors and always grateful for a glass of wine. But even then her remarks had a bitter edge to them that was depressing, if not actually frightening, to everyone in the house.

"I've lost my mind," she would say again and again in the course of an evening, and "It's sad, so sad"; "It's *evil*"; "My mind is gone"; "My mind isn't working right"—clichés that rang the changes of her melancholy moods, morbid clichés recited like slogans, with Pat's voice trailing off into the cheerless laughter of her humility and confusion.

Roald knew that it was the pregnancy and not some arbitrary sixth-month collapse that explained the slump in her attitude. Still, he couldn't deny being disappointed. It made him feel desperate to see good family friends like Jane Figg or Judy Knivett-Hoff or Marjorie Clipstone patiently waiting at the kitchen table for Pat to finish a second or third cup of coffee. They had come to the house for no other reason than to help her—these intelligent, devoted women, too kind to stop coming, too kind even to complain when it was obvious that Pat was bent on nothing more constructive than swindling another ten minutes away from the morning's work. Pat's teachers were totally reliable. They arrived at the house in strict accordance with the schedule Roald had posted on the kitchen bulletin board—three teachers for each morning and three more for the afternoon, giving Pat a full nine-to-six school day, with a three-hour break for lunch and a nap. They helped her with her reading and writing, and speech and memory and general mental agility. So very much remained to be done.

He was aware that Pat was suffering enough without being badgered, and according to the tenets of strict rehabilitation theory, he was probably not entitled to feel anything like frustration or disappointment, let alone display such feelings in sarcastic jibes and sallies. Early on, Pat had taken whatever he said in the cheerful and constructive way he meant it. "Come on, you great lump, you can't sit there in your chair all day . . ." and she would laugh along with him and struggle to her feet. But now his little jokes either went ignored or else rang false and a bit unpleasant, like nagging, or mocking, or powerless railings against this dreaded lassitude that had taken her off the job.

It had been easy enough to see the wisdom in canceling her sessions with the physiotherapist. Pat had become too ungainly for much exercise, and the therapist, a young flight surgeon at the RAF hospital nearby, was too chivalrous to bring any gusto to twisting and pulling the legs of a woman in her delicate condition. Perhaps the best thing would be to cancel the rest of the lessons as well, easing the pressure and letting Pat coast through the last dragging days of her pregnancy as comfortably as possible. Now that The Hawk had promised to advance the day, there wouldn't be all that much time lost. Two weeks—he supposed they could afford two weeks. And after Pat came home with the baby, her happiness and relief would bring her back to work at a pace that would make up in days for weeks of these dismal counterfeit lessons.

So that was it. He would call the ladies tomorrow and cancel all Pat's lessons. He glanced over at Pat, meaning to tell her, but Pat, with her head sharply bowed, was dozing.

Walking up the terrace toward the entrance, Pat saw Sarah and Jenny sitting at the kitchen table. Sarah was reading the *Daily Mirror,* Jenny a fan magazine. In the warm yellow light from the kitchen they looked like strangers in a library, absorbed in the pages lying open on the table. But Pat knew they were impatient for her news.

Sarah was twenty-two, five years older than Jenny, whose sparrow chest contained a heart that pulsed with the same yearnings so evident in Sarah. Sarah had become almost matronly out of all the sheer vicarious energy she put into her work, but both girls pined equally to be married, to be mothers, to share in all the rites that they lived to the hilt in their fantasies. At Gipsy House they were out of circulation, or nearly so; Sarah went to the Scotch dances in High Wycombe every other Wednesday night and Jenny had a boy friend named Jerry who called her up once in a while. They were "unsettled heifers," as Roald called them, and they had followed every development in Pat's pregnancy with an interest so avid that Sarah's face colored and Jenny's mouth went dry whenever the subject came up.

Jenny jumped to her feet when she heard Pat's footsteps at the door. The children came running from the nursery; they were fed and bathed and ready for bed. I snapped my notebook shut; Sarah cleared away the papers. "Good news from The Hawk," Roald said quietly as he passed by the table on his way to open a bottle of Beaujolais. This particular wine, a Fleurie he ordered by the case, was so good that he had been savoring it in sheer anticipation all the way back from Oxford. Pat bent down stiffly from the waist to hug the children, who then ran past her to cluster around Roald's legs.

"Ah . . . what did the doctor say, then, Mrs. Dahl?" Sarah asked, reddening slightly.

Pat had been waiting for someone to ask, and before answering, she looked at Sarah and then at Jenny with a delicious, mischievous grin. She hadn't had any news of her own in a while and she wanted to make the most of it. She's getting her timing back, Roald thought.

"He's going to . . . what's he going to do, Papa?"

"Induce—"

"Yes, induce. He's going to make it come two weeks before it's meant to."

"Oh, Mrs. Dahl, that's wonderful!" Jenny exclaimed. "Then you'll only have a few more weeks to wait."

"Even less," Roald replied. "It may be as early as next week."

"But how is it done?" Jenny asked. This was just the kind of obstetrical detail she thirsted to know.

"Drugs, Jenny," said Roald. "It's very easy and common."

Everyone murmured surprise and delight, and Pat beamed happily back, feeling well rewarded. Roald certified the occasion as one worth celebrating by pouring wine for Sarah and Jenny. Jenny usually turned it down, but this time she accepted. They raised their glasses and drank. Pat still had her coat on.

Sarah herded the children together for their good-night kisses, then coaxed them upstairs to bed. It was late for Theo and Ophelia. "Go up and tuck the nippers in, Pat," Roald said as soon as they had gone up. He had a way of cocking his head back and smiling when he made a suggestion like this. It was an indication that he was prepared to argue it.

"Good! A *splendid* idea. I'll do it." Pat put down her wineglass and followed the procession upstairs.

"Did you notice that?" Roald said in a voice meant to encourage agreement. "That's the first time in weeks that she's wanted to go. With the slightest bit of prodding, she bounces right back. Wait and see. When the baby comes we're going to see marvelous changes in Pat. We're going to see a great surging of the maternal instinct." Jenny smiled weakly and gulped.

Tessa was the first to bed. She had a room of her own above the nursery, with a bookshelf well stocked with novels about nurses and animals. Dolls meant very little to her and there were only one or two in the room. Instead, there were many small notebooks made of folded paper and marked "PRIVATE" in large, determined letters. "PROPERTY OF TESSA DAHL," they said, or "DIARY—KEEP OUT." Some of her papers were signed "Chantal Sophia Dahl," the name Pat and Roald had given her, then immediately thought better of. *Chantal Dahl*—the name was a mushy poem.

Tessa was already deep in a book when Pat came into the room. Her eyes flickered away from the page for a second when Pat bent down to kiss her.

"Good night, Teddy."

"Good night, Mummy."

Tessa looked up at her questioningly, then smiled and returned to her book. Pat went out, pulling the door shut behind her. "Don't close it, Mummy," Tessa called out. "I won't," said Pat, opening it a crack.

Pat knew she would have to win back her place in all the children's lives, but Tessa was the only one of them who was old enough to judge her, to feel sorry for her because her mind was no good any more, or ashamed of her—whatever it was that she felt. It was hard to tell whether Ophelia even realized that she was her mother, since Sarah fed her and changed her, and it was Sarah's bed she went to in the mornings. And Theo was so feverishly involved with living his supercharged life that her illness did not seem to affect him one way or another.

Roald was in the small bedroom Theo shared with Ophelia, showing his agent, who had come up from London for dinner, the collection of antique witch balls hanging on wires from the ceiling. They were hand-blown glass balls in all colors and sizes, some as big as cantaloupes, and they sparkled and shimmered like bubbles above the children's heads. Roald explained that in the early nineteenth century they were used to frighten witches away, and that finding this many, twenty or so, had taken years of fairly determined browsing.

"Read me a story, Daddy," Theo said from his bed.

"Not tonight, Titi. Your mother has just arrived to read to you."

"No, you do it, Daddy. Read me a *Peter Rabbit*."

"Yes, you do it," said Pat. "I don't feel like it."

"No, come on, try," Roald said. "You've got to get back to it."

Pat raised her eyebrows in elaborate resignation and sat down next to Theo on the bed. She chose a *Peter Rabbit* book and leaned back against the headboard so that Theo could follow the pale aquarelle drawings on every facing page. It was *The Tale of Pigling Bland,* and Pat read the title over several times before getting the "Pigling" right: "*The Tale of Pigling Bland,* by Beatrix Pott*ah*." Theo curled up to listen. Across the room, Ophelia was already asleep in her crib.

Pat read in a flat, uncomprehending voice, missing the point and stress of every sentence, studying each word with such severe concentration that the nail of the finger guiding her eye cut a fine, desperate scratch under each line of pudgy type. Sometimes a saccharine word or phrase came out with a strongly ironic inflection; she had learned to read again with *Peter Rabbit* as her text, and a large part of her hated these absurd, moralizing rodents whose naughty antics neither seemed funny nor gay but only reminded her of how abysmally she had slipped.

Theo squirmed and twitched in the bed beside her while Pat struggled on. She was wallowing in mid-paragraph now, ticking the words off with her finger, piling them up in the air with no sense of where they were leading and little memory of where they had begun. Roald stood by, helping her where he could but also adding to her anxiety, if only because he thought it best to stay, assuming that she'd get stuck. Theo yawned and twisted. Finally Pat threw down the book in exasperation.

"I don't understand one word," she moaned. "I haven't the slightest idea what I'm reading." She felt tears rising in her eyes.

"You mustn't worry about that," Roald said. *"Pigling Bland* is Potter's toughest book. It's not at all easy to follow."

He sounded as if he meant it, and so Pat sighed and plowed on. Before she had finished another page, Theo was asleep.

It was becoming a bitter thing for Pat to see her responsibilities pass her by. There were so few things within her range, and on bad days even these seemed to elude her. The children were almost wholly dependent on Sarah, and Roald had completely taken over the running of the house with the help of Mrs. Ingram, the housekeeper. And when Pat was urged and sometimes goaded into fighting to regain her role in the family, the immensity of the task seemed to overwhelm her, sending her back into the hopeless gallows humor of someone who knows that he is cursed. Recovery, it seemed, was something she dreaded as much as desired.

Pat told others a good many things she did not dare mention to Roald, because he did not suffer spasms of woe and self-pity very gladly, especially coming from Pat. He had too much at stake, all of it banked on her courage and endurance. However, I was in a different position; years of magazine interviewing had given me a knack for neutral listening. It was a talent, I knew, that I shared with bartenders and beauticians, and experience had taught me how unreliable the ramblings it induced could be. But when Pat, who is not a melodramatic person, began to talk about suicide, I sat up and listened.

At first she only made sad jokes about it. "I'd like to, but I don't know *how,*" she would say. Or, "Isn't it fine to be too dumb to kill yourself?" But as her mood darkened she spoke of it more often, adding rational touches that sounded almost like plans. "I'll wait until after the baby because now it wouldn't be fair." She asked how many sleeping pills it took, how many aspirin; hundreds, I told her, hoping that would put it out of reach. For days I debated telling Roald about it, not wanting to add to his worries but living with horrible fantasies in which my silence would brand me an accomplice to murder.

Then one night at supper Pat mentioned suicide in front of Roald and some guests, making her usual joke about not knowing how. She had drunk a bit too much wine, and the laughter that spilled out of her as she spoke sounded wild and demented. "Well, if that's all that's stopping you, your problems are solved," Roald said. "We've got knives in the kitchen that will do you up fine. And there are my razor blades upstairs. Or else you can lock yourself in the car and turn on the engine and before you know it, Bob's your uncle! Nothing to it!" His smile was fiercely disparaging. Pat grinned sheepishly and blinked adoring thank-yous across the table to Roald.

Roald drew me aside later that evening. I was worried that he wanted to discuss Pat's dangerous mood; I wouldn't know what to say. But instead he beckoned me over to a corner and said, "I've got something rather nice to show you." Ceremoniously he withdrew a small ring from his pocket.

"This is for Pat when she's had the baby," he said. "I bought it at Sotheby's a few weeks back."

The ring itself was a frail band of gold, and the oval bezel bore a fine engraving of a woman with a smaller object that appeared to be a sheaf of wheat. "Is it very old?" I asked.

"Fourth century B.C.," Roald said. "The bidding was stiff, I can tell you. I had to go a good bit higher than I'd planned. But it's Greek, you see, solid gold, and the engraving is still sharp and clear. Perfect condition, really."

"Who is the engraving of?" I asked, lifting the ring into the light. I was not sure that I had ever touched anything quite this old.

"It's Persephone," Roald replied, "the goddess of God-knows-what. It's quite beautiful, don't you think?"

"Yes, yes, I do. But you don't know who Persephone was?"

"Vaguely. I know the name. But I can't recall specifically what she did. We'll have to look it up."

The ring was the first thing that came to my mind when I

woke the next morning in my hotel room in London, and I decided to browse through the bookstores on Charing Cross Road before catching the train for Great Missenden. Roald would be pleased if I were to arrive with a full report on Persephone, daughter of Zeus and Demeter, the fertility goddess. The first mention I found of Persephone made me suck my teeth in dismay: "Bringer of destruction," it said. I leafed through half a dozen books, finding only passing references that confirmed the bad news: "Nymph of the River Styx"; "Her annual disappearance from the earth brought death to all vegetation"; "Dreaded and worshiped as 'The Maid,' whose name it was unwise to utter." She was abducted by Hades, then searched out by Demeter, who, wild with grief, brought a scourge to the fields wherever she wandered. Grapes on the vine withered into raisins, fruit dropped from the trees unripe. Zeus feared a famine that would finish man unless Demeter was appeased, so he sent Hermes to bargain with Hades for Persephone's return. But she was already compromised. She had eaten seven pomegranate seeds while in Hades' kingdom, and he demanded that she come back to spend a third of every year with him. This she did, acquiring Jekyll-and-Hyde powers as exterminating angel of the underworld and virginal protector of seedlings and sprouts, which emerged every year on the day of her return to her mother.

I was appalled. When Roald finds out about this, I thought, he won't dare give Pat the ring. The sheaf of wheat depicted on the ring took some of the sting out of it, suggesting that this was Persephone in her happier manifestation. (In Sicily, I had read, she was still honored as Cornucopia Queen.) She was, nevertheless, a dubious presence to attend the birth of a child—a schizophrenic goddess at the very best. I was sorry I had looked her up, and as I hailed a cab to the station I vowed that my lips would be sealed. If only it would slip Roald's mind—but then, that was most unlikely. In fact, it was odd that Roald hadn't already delved into the Persephone legend, considering the pleasure he always took in such expertise. It was highly uncharacteristic of him.

Not until an hour later, near the end of the train ride, was I struck with the certainty that Roald already knew. He had bought the ring, found out about Persephone and erased her from his mind. It was, after all, a beautiful ring.

⚙

"I've had to alert the press boys," Roald told the breakfast gathering on the day of Pat's departure for the hospital. "They've been calling all along, and I promised to let them in on it . . . So there will be a few photographers standing about in the lane when we leave for Oxford this afternoon. A.P. is coming, and U.P.I., and the Bucks *Free Press,* surely, and perhaps one or two London papers."

"The *Toimes,*" Pat suggested in her stagy English accent. Her spirits were high; it was a voice she used only when she wanted to be funny.

"The *Mail,* more likely, I should think," Roald said.

"Maybe *The People,* too," said Else, who had stopped by on her way home from the station.

"Yes, yes, I think *The People* wouldn't want to miss it."

Jenny and Sarah smiled across the table.

"What's so funny?" Pat asked, searching the four smiling faces. "What's the big joke?"

"The idea was, you see, Pat, that only the cheapest tabloids would be interested in your saga," Roald explained, drifting out into the kitchen to fill his morning thermos; in ten minutes more, he'd be working.

"Oh, Gawd," said Pat. "My brain is really gone, you know. I can't tell when people are being *bahstids* any more." Everyone collapsed with laughter while Pat looked around, feeling unaccustomed pride in her own good humor.

Pat's humor was a source of constant surprise. In ordinary conversation her comprehension was far better than her ability to express herself. But with jokes and banter it was just the other way around; she had far more trouble getting jokes than making them. The day before, I had spent an hour digging up cartoons in back issues of *The New Yorker*. I chose only those with no captions or with the simplest one-line gags, but Pat saw nothing funny in them. Of a cartoon showing a cannibal dressed in a suburbanite's "Genius At Work" barbecue apron and consulting a cookbook as he seasoned his missionary stew, Pat remarked, "Did he take what he's wearing from those people in the pot?"—a new and far crazier joke than I had seen, but not a source of any amusement to Pat. Of another cartoon, showing a fat mogul working on a rowing machine perched on the deck of his sleek cabin cruiser, Pat said, "He must be making it go."

Yet that same night at supper she had outfenced Roald with irony and finesse. They were sitting around the kitchen table, drinking coffee and sharing bars of "chockie" with the children.

"You're getting a bit long in the tooth, you know, Pat," Roald said pleasantly. "When you go into hospital to have this baby, I think I'll nip into London and find myself a girl—someone not quite so fossilized."

Pat answered with her wise, sleepy smile. "No girls, Papa," she said. "That wouldn't be good."

"Oh? Why not?"

"Because you might have a . . . heart attack."

Her mood had rebounded dramatically as soon as the date of the birth had been settled with The Hawk. The simple fact of having a definite appointment seemed to remove all the anxiety from her, and she astonished everyone with her energy and good disposition. She had gone through nearly a month of depression that concealed a great amount of progress, so that when her talk became animated and gay, it was rich in words and ideas that had been beyond her only a few weeks before.

Pat spruced herself up a bit for the photographers who would be coming that afternoon. She wore dark stockings and a kerchief, and a pale coat that billowed out around her like a shoplifter's special. It was raining, but she cheerfully went out to pose ten minutes before Roald was ready to leave. "I love anyone who will take my pic*tchah*," she told the photographers, and she looked as if she meant it, radiating genuine happiness as she obligingly struck poses under her umbrella. When Roald emerged from the house with her overnight case and a canvas bag containing boxes of the special Maryland cigarettes they smoked, writing pads, envelopes, post cards, stamps, pens, whiskey and gin, the photographers asked for a shot of him holding the car door while Pat eased herself into the seat. "A *splendid* idea!" Pat shouted in delight. "Come over here, Papa, and *ho-uld* my door." Roald grinned sheepishly at first, but then made a serious effort to maintain the pose until the cameras stopped clicking. "Thank you, thank you," said the photographers in a blur of deferential sounds. They backed away to their cars, waving and touching their rain hats. "What you have there is a collector's item," Roald told them as he got into the car. "It's the only picture in existence of me holding a door for Pat. I know that to be a fact because that was the first time since I've known her that I've done it."

"He's not kidding, either," Pat called out. "It's a good thing you did, making him."

Jenny and I climbed into the back; the plan was for us to stay in Oxford until after the birth, while Roald would drive back every evening to see the children to bed. Roald's sisters helped Sarah bring Tessa and Theo out into the rain to say good-bye one last time. They all laughed and waved as the car pulled away. Theo danced around in a circle, throwing kisses with both hands in all directions. And because Roald held the car to a very slow roll while he wiped off steam on the windshield with his sleeve, it seemed that Theo's piping voice followed us far, far down the lane: "G'-bye! G'-bye!"

It was an hour's drive to Oxford, made longer by the rain and by rain-water lakes that the storm had laid into hollows and dips in the road. The day's happy mood stayed with us and we hardly bothered to talk. Several times during the slow, winding drive across the Chiltern Hills, Pat turned around in her seat and patted Jenny or me on the knee. There was such strength and affection in the way she did it that Jenny grasped her hand and held it, and I had to struggle to stifle my impulse to reach over and hug her for all I was worth. Roald sucked thoughtfully on his pipe. The windshield wipers thumped heavily back and forth.

The expressway into Oxford was so flooded that passing trucks kicked up huge rooster trails of muddy water and we pulled off on the shoulder to let the traffic pass. Pat grew edgy as we waited.

"Are you all right?" Roald asked.

"Oh, Papa, I don't know," she said. "I'm afraid about birthing this baby. I'm afraid the baby's going to have a reformed . . . face."

Roald answered, with the thinnest possible laugh, "You mean 'deformed,' Pat, but you're wrong. That isn't going to happen."

Then we splashed down the hill into Oxford, creeping through the town in a crush of heavy traffic.

"Tell me, Jenny," said Roald, "have you ever—how shall I put it?—stayed in a hotel by yourself before?"

"No, Mr. Dahl," said Jenny.

"Ah, well then, Jenny, you're in for an unforgettable experience. Anything can happen in a hotel, you know. You've got to keep your wits about you."

"Yes, Mr. Dahl," Jenny said.

"You're prepared to deal with the succubus, or rather, the incubus?"

"Yes, Mr. Dahl," Jenny said, blushing happily. She had been through this routine before.

Roald had found a "safe" but nevertheless charming hotel for Jenny to stay in while Pat remained in the hospital. That way Pat would have someone with her all day long, and Jenny could help with the correspondence. But the assignment to Oxford was intended as a reward for Jenny as much as a service to Pat. Roald was fond of Jenny and she appealed mightily to his Pygmalion streak. She was barely seventeen—unformed clay, a girl from the emptiest, most troubled kind of background. Roald used to say that her accent alone was enough to condemn her to a life in one of the council houses—those vast prisons for the luckless and unambitious that passed for low-income housing projects. If she only had sense enough to stay with them they could do her a great deal of good. The trouble was that these "unsettled heifers" weren't content with the quiet life. They had to go out every night with some twerp who had a motorbike. Jenny's dream was to be a shopgirl in High Wycombe, for God's sake—simply so she could "meet people." As if she wasn't meeting people now.

Lucy Neal Dahl was born at 8:23 the next morning, August 4, 1965, one hundred and sixty-nine days after Pat's stroke. Roald and I, dressed in surgical masks and gowns, were in the delivery room seconds later, together with Leonard McCombe, *Life* magazine photographer, who nimbly climbed a tower of chairs to beam in on Pat's face from above. Except for Olivia, who was born in New York, all the children had been delivered by the same friendly hands, and The Hawk stood by in expansive good humor as hospital discipline collapsed all around him. "Could we have one with the baby now?" Leonard called down. Nesta Powell, a senior nurse at the clinic and a close family friend, laid the small bundle in the crook of Pat's right arm so that Pat, rising up on her good left arm, could glimpse the pinched red face deep inside the blanket.

"Oooo, Lucy, you're my *last* baby," she cooed, her fingers stitching protectively along the hem of the blanket. "You're good and you're fine and you're my last baby."

Pat's labor had lasted less than four hours and the birth

was easy and uncomplicated. "It wasn't like birthing a baby at all," Pat kept saying. She felt fresh and euphoric, and against the white hospital linen her face looked radiant and suffused with healthy color. During the summer I had almost forgotten what a beauty Pat was. It was her mood, some clue to her feelings, that I had searched for in her face, but found pain and the nearness of death there—above all, loneliness, a loneliness that defied me to look more deeply. But seeing Pat now, this joyous, glowing, intensely beautiful woman, I realized that I had thought of her as ravaged and wounded until this moment. I had often seen Pat smile as broadly as this, but it was always as though she were *smiling through*. Now her smile was no longer courageous; it was a triumphant smile, the first one I had seen.

"You look marvelous, Pat," I said.

"I tell you I feel wonderful," she said. "I can't remember when I've felt so good. It really was not at all like birthing a baby."

Sleeping pills were decreed all the same, and after Nesta had wheeled Pat back to her room, Roald quizzed Dr. Hawksworth very closely. "Absolutely nothing to worry about," the doctor said from behind his half-moon glasses. "Nothing whatever to worry about, absolutely nothing at all. We had a moment or two there because of the foetus' position; a bit curled around, you know, but really nothing out of the ordinary. Simple enough, everything fine, the baby fine, a good size, no lumps or bruises. Just the tiniest scrape on one cheek. But nothing, really—a perfect baby. Your wife, as you saw, feels fine. It couldn't have gone better."

"What about the cheek?"

"Oh, that's just a small scrape, gone in a week with no trace. The baby's head is perfectly formed, unusually so, really. Rather serene. And terribly pretty, of course."

I called the newspapers and wire services while Roald called his sisters and his mother ("Of course!" she said. "I told you it would be a girl months ago!"), and then sent telegrams to Pat's mother, her Aunt Maude, and a few friends in Los Angeles and New York. We ate a quick lunch before Roald spoke to a gathering of reporters who had come up from London to cover the birth. He was elegant and relaxed and he talked on longer than he had meant to, with the reporters laughing encouragingly in all the right places and taking copious notes.

Pat still had another two hours to sleep by the time they were finished, so Roald took me on a walk around town. Roald was no academician, much less an Oxonian, but he had never regretted choosing to forgo the university. After school he had gone to Africa, which was an education and a fine old time, signing chits in smart British clubs, playing unbeatable golf, prattling with the blacks in Swahili—a life from the pages of Somerset Maugham. But his accent and manner belonged to streets like these, and strolling around Oxford, he seemed as comfortable as an old don. The very names of the colleges, as Roald pointed them out, rang with liturgical importance in my ear: *All Souls, St. John's, Magdalen, Christ Church.*

Roald was tired and bone-sore when we started on our walk, but the pleasure of having some time to kill was unfamiliar and heady, and soon he was outpacing me, pushing ahead eagerly, looking into every shop. At a bootmaker's he elicited a fascinating discourse on the art of how to last shoes and on the qualities of leather. Then, at a pet store in the market, he learned how to sex a tortoise (females have flat chests; males, concave) and bought one to bring home to Theo. He found a witch ball for Tessa in an antique shop he knew, and at a rare-book dealer's he pressed upon me an 1840 medical text called *Observations on the Testicles.* "Take it," he said. "You never know when you might need to look something up."

Pat was sitting up in bed, drinking beer and playing dominoes with Jenny when Roald and I returned to the hospital. She still looked rosy and exultant, and her room was already crowded with flowers. Without a hint of ceremony, so inconspicuously that neither Jenny nor I saw him do it, Roald gave Pat the Greek gold ring. He chuckled contentedly at her yelps of delight and briefly submitted to a bear hug. Pat put the ring on the little finger of her left hand and gazed at it with glistening eyes while Roald looked on, still chuckling in a quiet, embarrassed way. Then he proposed a drink, and we settled down to a long conversation that consisted mainly of rolling Lucy's name over our tongues; it was a pretty name, which the parents were proud of—Lucy Neal Dahl. With Olivia, they had gone perhaps just a step too far, giving her the middle name of "Twenty" for no reason other than the beauty of the word. "Tessa" they praised as a smooth recovery from their foolish choice of "Chantal," and they raved about "Theo" and "Ophelia"—solid, pretty names which were unique without being the least bit recherché. But "Lucy Neal" was in many ways the best name of the lot. It would ring firm and true on both sides of the ocean, and using the Neal family name would be manna to

Pat's mother. The mention of Mrs. Neal reminded them that this would be a good time to call. By the time the transatlantic connection was made, Pat had grown tired and her mother had already heard the news on television. But "Lucy Neal" went over just as well as they knew it would.

Roald came to the hospital every afternoon to see the baby and sit with Pat until she was ready for sleep. "Just answer the really nice ones from cozy old people you don't know," he told her as they opened the stacks of cards and letters and telegrams. "Your friends don't expect you to write."

"All right, Papa," Pat would say, but the rule was difficult to follow because so many of her friends' names were strange and unfamiliar. "Do we know this one, Papa?"

"Yes, of course, Pat, you remember . . ."

But sometimes she could not remember.

The mail had started arriving in bundles the day after Lucy was born. Some was from fans who make a hobby of her. "Hi, Pat!" these happy people began, and they told her of their Pat Neal scrapbooks and her autographed picture hanging over their beds. There were extravagant words and gestures—a telegram that read: "YOU ARE A SOURCE OF INSPIRATION FAR GREATER THAN ANY RELIGIOUS LEADER STOP." "Good man!" was Pat's comment when she read it. But most of the mail came from ordinary people who simply could not restrain themselves. They had to write a first, shy letter, if only to say "Good luck to you" or "God spare you more grief."

The birth seemed to release Pat's friends from the inhibitions caused by their worry. Nearly everyone was heard from, and many explained their silence through the summer by saying that up until now they hadn't known quite what to say. It was a feast of pride and affection, and Pat reveled in it, shamelessly asking that the purplest tributes be read aloud time and again. "Now, *that* one really knows what he's talking about," she would say. Or, more innocently, "Isn't she a beautiful writer?"

Roald was the only one to disturb her idyll. For months he had been looking forward to her being able to walk when she no longer had to carry the baby, and now he could wait no longer. He had had the brace removed from her police matron's shoes, and he was lacing them on her feet two days after Lucy's birth. "I don't know about this, Papa," Pat said. "I feel kind of . . . shaky."

"Nonsense," said Roald. "It's just this lotus-eater life you're leading. You'll be fine as soon as you start."

Pat's first unaided steps without the brace were feeble and halting. She would lift one foot, then plant it, like a marionette's, each step landing on the brink of a fall. Roald was right behind her in the corridor, urging her on like a drill instructor, "Don't limp! It's not onetwo, threefour, onetwo, threefour. It's one, two, three, four; one, two, three, four. Stride out! Stride out!"

[illegible] more [illegible] brown quite when [illegible] the purplest [illegible] heater [illegible] said, "Oh, [illegible]," [illegible] warm?"

Ronald was the only one to distract her now. For months he had been [illegible] to her [illegible] when she no longer had to [illegible], and now he could wait no longer. He had had the brace removed from her polio [illegible] shoe, and [illegible] her [illegible] two days after Lucy's birth. "I don't know about this, Papa," Pat said. "I'm kind of . . . shaky."

"Nonsense," said Ronald. "It's just the [illegible] life [illegible]. You'll be fine as soon as [illegible]."

Pat's first [illegible] the [illegible] were feeble and [illegible] one foot, then plant it, like a [illegible], each [illegible] on the brink of a fall. Ronald was right behind her in the corridor, [illegible] on like a drill [illegible]. "Don't [illegible]! It's not [illegible], therefore [illegible]. It's one, two, three, four; one, two, three, four. Shoulders [illegible] out!"

6

GIPSY HOUSE looked like a construction site when Pat came home from the hospital. Roald was having a two-story wing built to join the main house with the guest house behind it, and there was also cabinet work to be done in the kitchen, plus an inside wall that needed moving "to give the nursery some character." Hoping to have both kitchen and nursery ready as a welcoming surprise for Pat, he had hired not only the trusted Wally, who had worked on the house a dozen times already, but also a crew of three "general men," as Wally dryly referred to his staff. But Roald should have recalled from earlier projects that Wally's approach to his work entailed great amounts of meditation—long intervals several times a day when hammers fell silent and the crew stood by, watching Wally sight in angles and perspectives over the rim of his teacup. The confusion lasted for days, causing Mrs. Ingram to resign in protest after ten years' daily service. The house was ankle-deep in sawdust and scattered tools when Pat came in the door.

The children rushed up to have a look at Lucy. Tessa, taller than her brother by a foot, was just the right height to nuzzle ecstatically against the small sphere of down that showed from the top of Pat's bundle; Theo stood on tiptoe and tugged impatiently at the blanket until Sarah came and dragged him away; Don-mini, who somehow seemed to know exactly what her mother had brought back, stood at Pat's feet, clinging to her skirt with one hand while the other reached up to touch the blanket with a pointing finger. "Baby! Baby!" she cooed.

"Oh, God—watch out!" Pat shouted, anxious about her footing. "Watch out! Get back . . . *Ophelia!* Gawd. I'll show you, I'll *show* you. Roald! *Rooo*-ald! Come in here and take this baby." Roald lifted Lucy out of her arms; Pat turned and limped heavily into the safety of the living room. Outside, men lunged past the windows with heavy piles of bricks on their backs.

"Mummy! Your brace is gone!" said Tessa, stopping short in wonderment.

"Yes, Teddy, isn't that good?"

"Oh, yes, Mummy, how super!"

"The brace is gone! Mummy's brace is gone!" Theo sang out, racing back to the nursery to bring the news to Sarah.

Else and her twins had turned up, and Marjorie Clipstone was now in possession of Lucy, holding her carefully with unpracticed hands while the women and children crowded around her chair, cooing and clucking adoringly.

"You would never-ever know that I was the one who

birthed him, would you?" Pat said. Her tone was lightly ironic.

"You mean 'her,' " someone said.

"Her! When *will* I stop doing that?"

"You don't do it so much any more, Pat," said Marjorie.

"Oh, Jesus—yes, I do. Sometimes I can't even think of—*her* name. Her name is *Lucy . . . Neal . . . Dahl."* She pronounced each name with an actress's flair, projecting her voice to the back of the hall.

"Lovely name, Pat"; "Such a pretty name"; "I love the name," said Marjorie, Else, the twins and Angela, who had just come in from a game of tennis.

"So happy you like it!" Pat said, bursting into inexplicable laughter. "My mother *loves* it. She likes the 'Neal' best, but she likes 'Lucy,' too."

"In the South they would always call her 'Lucy Neal,' " I said. *"Lucy Neal! Git on in heah an' eat yo grits."*

"That's *true,"* said Pat, as though dealing in revelation. "I was always 'Patsy Louise' until I went to college. That's my real name. Pat-*ree*-cia is something I thought up later." Again she laughed, wrinkling her nose and rocking forward over her folded arms.

The company agreed that Lucy resembled Theo and Olivia, the dark-eyed, dark-haired strain in the family that most closely resembled Pat; Tessa and Don-mini were fair-skinned, blue-eyed and blond, like Roald's sisters and all their children. When Lucy woke up, still in Marjorie's lap, everyone rejoiced in the fullness of her peeps and squeaks, and tender hands reached out to scoop her up into various posture norms of baby comfort: lifted high up on the shoulder, cradled and rocked in the arms, cuddled and pressed against a swaying chest, none of which had any effect at all.

"I think she is trying to tell you something," said Roald, who had been sitting in a neutral corner nursing a drink.

"She says she would appreciate her *suppah,*" Pat said. "She would think it was a very good thing if I gave her her *suppah.*"

"In that case, perhaps a friendly game of bowls," said Roald, rising and massaging the small of his back in a dignified, barrel-stave stretch. I followed him out to the toolshed, where the teakwood balls were stored in their box. A spate of fine weather was upon us, and the lawn was firm and dry for the first time since early summer. Roald let the heavy balls fall onto the grass, but before we could begin he was overcome by his obsession to mow.

"Can't play in this stuff," he said, distastefully fingering the shaggiest patch, which was no more than three quarters of an inch long. He went back into the rugosa-covered shed for the gasoline mower. "One quick run 'round will do it nicely," he added as he pushed the machine out into the sunshine. *Kaf, kaf, kaf, ku-haf, ku-haf*—no luck in ten minutes of trying. "To hell with it, I can do it just as quickly with the old one"—and he wheeled out the unfailing hand mower. He mowed at the speed of normal walking, starting at the flower-edged perimeter and moving nonstop in concentric circles that finally brought him to the herbaceous border around the dogwood at the center of the lawn; hugging the delphinium rail, he finished in a fast, tight circle, then peeled off and mowed his way back into the shed. The grass was now the length of a GI haircut; to me the lawn looked punished, if not actually defoliated—it had lost its verdant depth.

"Right, then," said Roald. "What shall it be? Eleven the game? Shilling a point?"

"Half crown," I suggested. I was trying to get even.

"Are you sure? It could cost you two and a half pounds, you know."

"I know, or you just as easily. So a half crown, plus ten shillings for winning."

"Oh, dear—now we really are getting into it. Suppose we make it a ten-shilling bonus if you win by five, and five shillings for winning by less."

"Okay. Who goes first?"

"We flip." Roald flipped; tails, I won. We had played so often during the summer that I knew the wens and furrows in the rolling lawn almost as well as Roald; my string of losses was due to inferior concentration and technique, or so Roald said. I placed the jack—the small target ball—on a cresting rise just above the lily bed and returned to the starting line near the shed. I picked up the first ball and tried to let myself melt into the stooped orang-utan posture of the veteran bowler addressing his pitch. With a fine pendulum swing of the arm I sent the ball spinning on a thirty-foot arc that brought it within a few inches of the jack.

"Ah, you're mean as buggery today, aren't you?" Roald said, stepping up to the line. Tall though he was, and slightly stiff-legged, Roald played the game gracefully, setting the wooden ball on a smooth, spinning roll with a long sweep of his arm. His shot spun out and carried all the way to the jack, nudging mine aside. He strode across the lawn to examine the lay. "I'm afraid you'll be depressed to hear that I'm touching the *cochonnet!*" he called out happily from across the lawn.

Roald scored a point on the first series, then set up a tricky shot that ran back into a hollow near the shed. We played it, then another, moving at a slow, evening pace. It was fine to be there, playing this gentle game. The garden was in abundant bloom again, circling the lawn with deep beds of roses. A gaily decorated gypsy caravan stood on high spoked wheels at the top of the garden near a rail fence that enclosed a large, grassy apple orchard. Flocks of budgerigars streaked across the lawn to a corner by the lane where there was a beautiful aviary; fifty years ago it might have served as a gazebo at Deauville. Despite all the work going on in and around the house, it still looked serene and graceful, a rambling old house covered so thickly with roses that the door seemed like the portal to an arbor. Suddenly Sarah appeared in the doorway and shouted that someone wanted Roald on the telephone. "Tell them I'll call back in a half-hour," he told her, without asking who it was.

"You've seen how Pat lacks confidence with the children," Roald reflected.

He leaned forward and sent a ball skidding across the grass. "She's terrified of not being a proper mother to Lucy. She can't trust herself to carry the baby around, of course, and she can't even change her nappy."

"You don't think she's giving up, do you?"

"Oh, no, not Pat. Pat is a splendid, courageous and humble girl. The marvelous cheerfulness she had in California is gone now, and this past month hasn't been much good. But there's no question about her will when it comes to the family. I think she could accept giving up her career. Since Olivia's death she's lost any desperate will to succeed. Things like that cost you something, you know. You lose most of the egotism, the desire to get things for yourself, including success and ambition. Pat was very happy to get the Oscar and put in a good performance. But there's no driving ambition there. If it came to that, she'd be able to let the career go without any tremendous wrenching. There would be sadness about it, but nothing more. The intolerable thing is to lose her place in the family."

He fell silent as we took our turns bowling. I won two points on the pitch, but Roald was still ahead. He scored the game's last point just as Theo came sweeping across the lawn in a robin suit someone had given him for his fifth birthday a few weeks before. The suit had brown tights, a brown cotton helmet covering his head and neck, and a scarlet-bibbed jumper with a scalloped cape that billowed behind his outstretched arms to form two vague, fluttering wings. It was Theo's dream to go unnoticed among the birds, and he circled past the aviary in the robin disguise, looking back over his shoulder to see how the budgies were taking it. We watched him sail lightly over the lawn, running in his slightly oblique way, the right foot landing tentatively. Roald followed him with tender eyes. "Theo really is a lot of fun," he remarked with his quiet chuckle. Then his thoughts returned to the game.

"Well, now—eleven-five, was it? I'm afraid this is going to cost you dearly. Six points at a half crown, plus the bonus, makes . . . oh, dear—one pound, five shillings. Shall I put it on account?"

"No, no, I'll pay," I said, fishing in my pockets.

"Daddy! Daddy!" Theo shouted as he ran past. "Look how fast I can go. Do you see, Daddy?"

"Yes, Titi, we're watching every move."

Theo raced down to the guest-house windows, danced there in mockery of his dancing reflection, jeering "Nyeah, nyeah, nyeah" at the glass, then charged back up the sloping lawn, laughing in gasps, eyes askew, skipping in a three-beat step and flapping his elbows against his sides in a pantomime that came across less as a robin trot than as horse and rider, the Pony Express. It was only in the past few months that Theo had been able to run like this without lacing panic through his parents' hearts. He flung himself against Roald's legs, panting victoriously.

"Can you teach me to fly if I've got this suit on, Daddy?" Laughter still bubbled out of him, but his head was cocked for a true-life answer.

"Well, Titi, I don't know. We'll have to wait for a windy day."

Roald sat up late that night composing a memo to Pat's team of amateur therapists, who would be coming again in the morning after nearly a month's absence. He had built up tremendous respect for these helpers and he took an almost aesthetic pleasure in seeing so willingly realized the old ideal of townspeople helping one another. It had taken only a half-dozen phone calls to book Pat up for a week.

Ordinarily, Roald refrained from giving advice, preferring to let the tutors work out their own ideas with Pat and one another. That way each of them brought her own talents

ABOVE: Roald and his sisters, 1925. Behind him Asta; on his left, Else; and Alfhild is on his right. If they were to strike the same pose today, the closeness between them would be just as evident.
FROM THE DAHLS' COLLECTION

ABOVE RIGHT: Roald in the RAF, the Middle East, 1940. Roald's air service was brief but "very busy," as the Air Ministry modestly put it: he had eighty hours of combat against the Germans, Italians and Vichy French, and scored a couple of kills before he crashed and was put on the disabled list.
FROM THE DAHLS' COLLECTION

LEFT: Pat in a still from *The Fountainhead,* her first big Hollywood picture (though her second picture, in fact). Hollywood tried to make Pat into a glamour queen rather than utilize her talent, and the image never took. Here she is, lithe and alluring at twenty-two.

ALLAN GRANT—*Life* MAGAZINE © TIME INC.

RIGHT: Gary Cooper and Pat in *The Fountainhead,* in the climactic scene where the simple tradesman reacts as any ordinary man would, with a classic movie clinch that stops her fists from flailing at his chest.

ALLAN GRANT—*Life* MAGAZINE © TIME INC.

BELOW: Pat and Paul Newman in her Oscar-winning performance in *Hud,* unquestionably Pat's best picture, the only one in which her natural beauty and naturally beautiful manner are allowed to emerge intact.

SY FRIEDMAN—PARAMOUNT

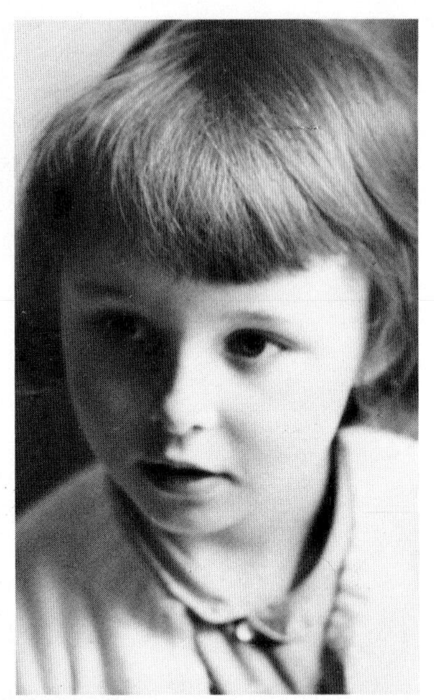

LEFT: Olivia at age six, two years before her death. She filled a perfect role in the family's country life: she could paint and make up poems and had an irresistible sense of humor, but the rarest thing about her was her love of nature.

FROM THE DAHLS' COLLECTION

BELOW LEFT: Theo, aged five, in the summer of Pat's stroke, at Gipsy House.

FROM THE DAHLS' COLLECTION

BELOW: The Dahls at the Los Angeles airport before going home to England three months to the day after Pat's stroke. "I feel fine," Pat told reporters, but the picture speaks for itself. The baby in Pat's lap is Ophelia; Tessa stands behind Roald, and Theo sits on his lap.

AP WIREPHOTO

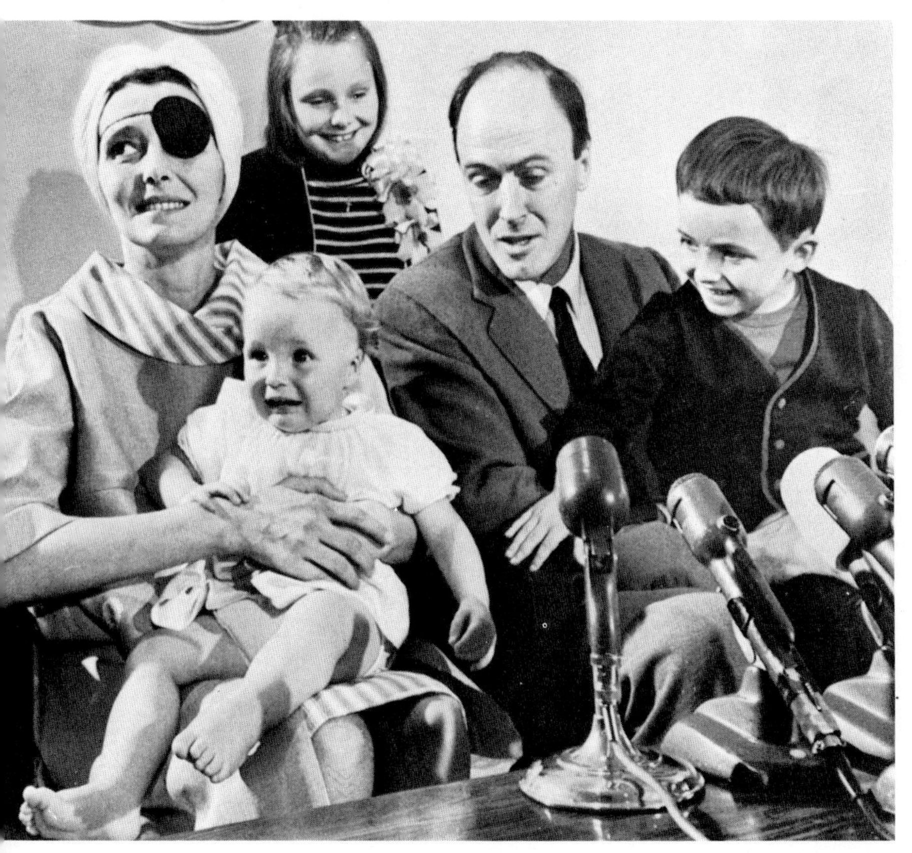

ABOVE: Pat and Angela Kirwan (the close family friend who often came to Gipsy House to help Pat in the months following her return to England). Here Angela gives the sound to a word Pat's tracing finger has found in the text of a child's storybook. Summer 1965.

LEONARD MCCOMBE—*Life* MAGAZINE © TIME INC.

LEFT: Pat in the summer of 1965 relearning to walk without her leg brace at the RAF hospital in Halton, a village ten miles or so from Great Missenden. The therapist is an RAF flight surgeon named Hugh MacDougal.

LEONARD MCCOMBE—*Life* MAGAZINE © TIME INC.

NEXT PAGE: Roald reads a fan letter as Pat looks on at the kitchen table in Gipsy House. Handwriting was especially difficult for her, and Roald read all the mail aloud for nearly a year. Summer 1965.

LEONARD MCCOMBE—*Life* MAGAZINE © TIME INC.

203
CFC

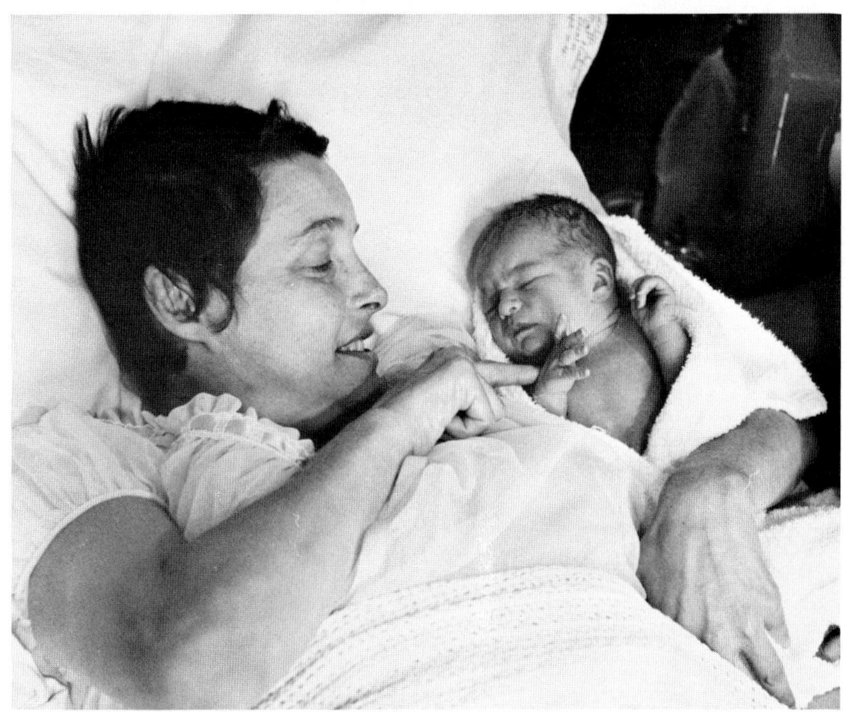

ABOVE: Pat with Lucy Neal a few minutes after her birth, still inside the delivery room. The relief Pat felt when she discovered that her baby was perfect released a great store of vitality and good humor. August 1965.

LEONARD MCCOMBE—*Life* MAGAZINE © TIME INC.

LEFT: Pat and Roald on an outing to Oxford, a week or so before the birth of Lucy. The heavy pregnancy, together with her shorn hair and leg brace, made Pat despair of her appearance until after the baby was born.

LEONARD MCCOMBE—*Life* MAGAZINE © TIME INC.

ABOVE: Tessa reads a mushy fan magazine's rave for the Beatles while Pat listens and struggles to understand. Pat would often be full of praise for the mastery of the reader—without having a single clue to what she had just heard.

LEONARD MCCOMBE—
Life MAGAZINE © TIME INC.

RIGHT: Roald teaching Theo the proper gentle approach to budgies, two of which have been brought in from the aviary. Even at the busiest, maddest and most depressing times, Roald had a marvelous capacity to get into any subject at all with the children.

LEONARD MCCOMBE—
Life MAGAZINE © TIME INC.

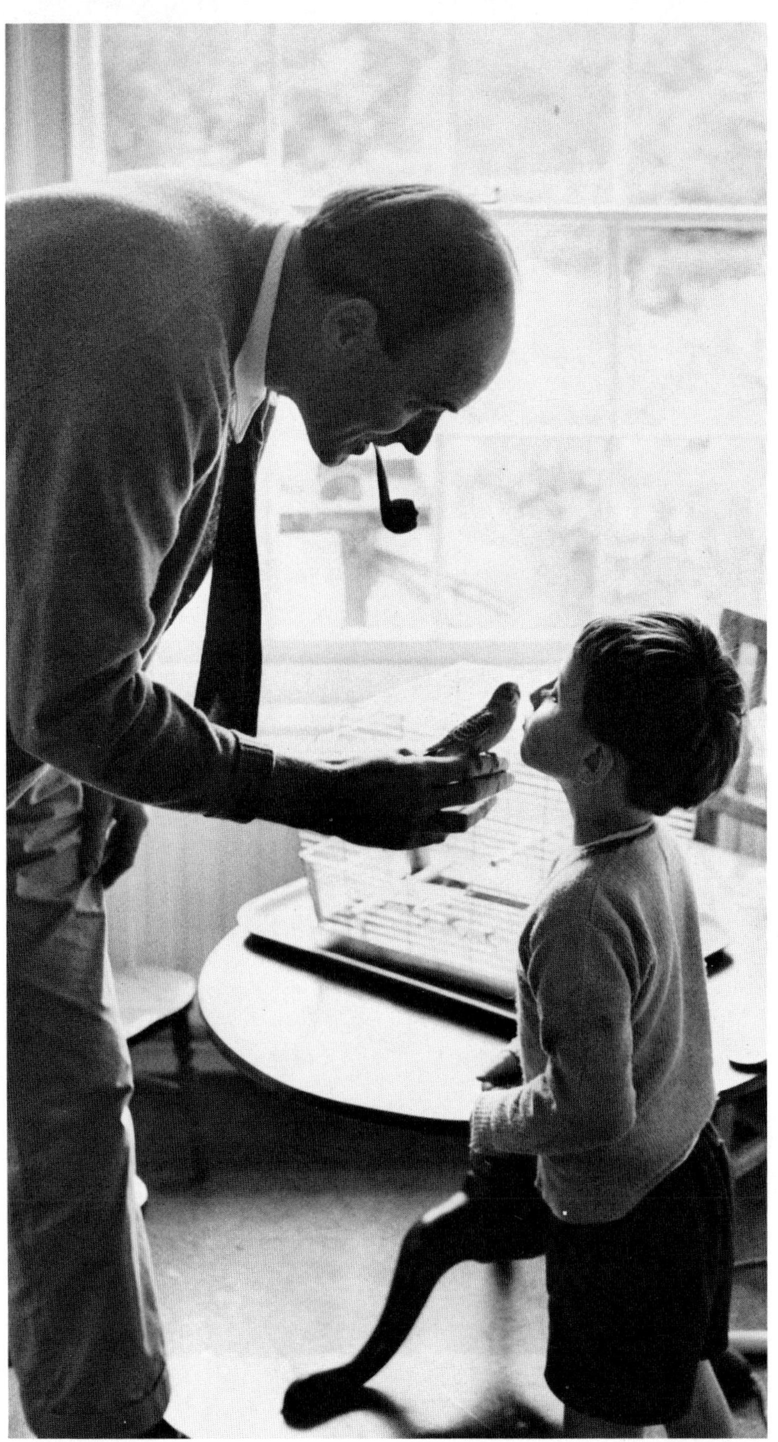

Pat at the "Evening with Patricia Neal" at the Waldorf in March 1967, giving her big speech to a ballroomful of friends and important presences. She approached the speech with tremendous apprehension, then delivered it with a confidence that simply came to her as she stepped out from the wings.

LEONARD MCCOMBE—*Life* MAGAZINE © TIME INC.

Pat receives her Heart of the Year award from President Johnson at a ceremony in the oval office. Pat went to the White House jauntily dressed in a blue suit and bright green boots. February 1, 1968.

WALTER BENNETT—TIME INC.

Pat on the set of *The Subject Was Roses*, the film in which she made her return to the screen after three years of convalescence from her stroke. The hard work sharpened her and revived her confidence in herself, and her director was full of compliments for her. Her dressing room was crowded with photographers and newspapermen, and nearly every day someone or other felt inspired to send her a dozen red roses, so that she was rarely without them through the ten winter weeks that she worked.

and ingenuity into play, making the scope of the lessons broad and imaginative. From the kitchen he had heard them going at it, and he was amazed at how skillfully they worked to strike a spark in Pat. When her mood was right, Pat was a most rewarding pupil, and the tutors all seemed as gratified by working with her as she was grateful to them for doing it. He only regretted that he had not thought of recruiting friends in Los Angeles to supplement the work of the professional speech therapist. The therapist had come only an hour a day, five days a week, costing a small fortune and leaving Pat with far too much idle time. It was true that her condition at the time would not have permitted a very full schedule. But surely one or two amateurs tossed in with the pro would have done no harm at all.

Roald meant the memo to give Pat's tutors some idea of her progress in the time since they last saw her so that the lessons could get off to a fast, encouraging start. But once he put his mind to it, he discovered that it was almost impossible for him to recall exactly how Pat had been a month before. The one dramatic change had been shucking the leg brace; the rest was as subtle as the advance of the seasons, a process you weren't aware of until it had already happened. And yet he was positive that she had made significant gains, despite her idleness and anxiety and struggles with dejection. The simple pressures of living were themselves constant tutors, and every passing day brought further mending to her brain.

He judged that her recovery was already sixty or seventy percent complete. There had been the wondrous transition from helplessness into a kind of primitive intelligence expressed in smiles and grimaces and cave-man sounds. That, in turn, had evolved into a period of swift rediscovery in which Pat acquired a childlike aura that was marvelous and touching and, as he recalled, filled with comic moments. Then, imperceptibly, that had given way to this unhappy time just past. Melancholy was the enemy, and it had slowed Pat's progress. But, in perspective, it might also have served as the vehicle for her returning awareness. It was, after all, an emotion entirely appropriate to her circumstance, and seeing her blue, one sensed that she was appraising herself at depths she could not have reached a few months before. Now, hopefully, a new change would emerge as the possibility of a complete recovery became more real to her, and as she, in the accumulation of healing days, became increasingly able to live up to it.

Only Pat seemed to have had no sensation of making any forward movement. To her, the pace was hatefully slow. She was always amazed when people who had been away for a few weeks or months raved about how radically she had improved. "Really? Really?" she would say with delight—but there remained something incredulous in her eyes. The difficulty in charting her improvement was that her new facility in speech did not always imply gains in comprehension and, more often, improved comprehension stayed trapped behind a tongue that could not find the words it knew.

The trick was to keep coming up with things that would interest her without being so difficult that she came away discouraged. At this point, *Peter Rabbit* was obviously out. But which books could you count on not to insult the intelligence of a mature woman whose reading level was somewhere below Tessa's? They had tried Hemingway because of the short sentences and plain language, but the complexity of the ideas was still defeating. Besides, Pat had never been a great novel reader—or even a reader of Great Novels. If you asked her if she had read Dickens or Thackeray, the answer was likely to be no. Perhaps newspapers were as good as anything. The short lines would help keep her eye from straying, and the fact of concentrating hard on some news story could bring a double benefit, sharpening both her reading and her awareness of the world. If only the bloody things weren't so badly written. Still, Roald thought it vital that she be reminded at every turn that the world was going to keep spinning, with or without her. "The fact of being ill doesn't place you at the center of the universe," he would tell her. It was natural enough for an invalid to become an egomaniac, but Pat was no invalid any more and she wasn't going to get away with becoming an egomaniac, either. So newspapers then, and perhaps brief discussions of major events—he put the idea down in his memo.

There would be no further point in working on enunciation. The slightly drunken slur had disappeared from her voice, and she spoke as clearly as ever. She affected something of an ersatz accent at times, but that was enjoyable and interesting. Having relearned English in England, the old Kentucky girl now sounded like someone who had grown up on the Tennessee-Buckinghamshire border. It would be marvelous, though, if the tutors could help her work away from the need to talk so much in formulas. She still said "That'll be good" a hundred times a day, and lately her talk had become larded with all sorts of elaborate space fillers. "I'm very sorry to have to tell you . . . that I'm going up to take a bath"; "It would be a very good thing . . . if we had a cup of coffee." This kind of jargon had a rather appealing, old-fashioned ring, and using it gave her little oases of security in almost every sentence. She could hold the floor a shade longer without fear of a mistake. But ultimately it became comically repetitious, like saying *"Ah, très bien"* all the time to conceal your ignorance of French. "Don't allow her to take refuge in pat phrases," he wrote, smiling at the well-used pun.

He wasn't sure about the value of memorizing poetry. It was a good exercise for her memory and she had slaved at it before.

Bright star, would I were stedfast as thou art—

. . .

Still, still to hear her tender-taken breath,
And so live ever—or else swoon to death.

But without much notion of poetic meaning, even after it was explained to her, she had to rely on learning the words by rote, and her memory wasn't up to it. Sometimes she would reverse or omit words or whole lines and go on with no awareness of having made a shambles of it. More often she would simply draw a blank, and with fists clenched in fury she would press her wrists against her temples in a gesture of boundless frustration. "It's gone, it's gone," she would say at last, breaking off the lesson with the saddest and most dangerous of all her clichés. "I'm through acting. *I can't remember lines."*

It was important to push her to the limits of her intellect, and that inevitably led her to the point of failure. But it was a poor idea to cause her to encounter failure too often. Perhaps they should forgo the poetry and instead find a few simple passages of dialogue from plays she'd done in the past. That way she would have both recollection and conversational logic to buttress pure memory work. He put down the suggestion with a question mark. The teachers would know as well as he did what to do.

❂

"All the shops are *closed!* All the curtains *drawn!* All the doors are *locked!* All the people *gone!*" Tessa, Theo and Roald chanted their ritual chant as they drove through the dark and empty High Street on their way home from a long afternoon spent shopping for school uniforms in London. Tessa would be going back to Godstowe in High Wycombe, a small snooty school preparatory for the big snooty schools, but she had outgrown last year's kit and needed everything new. Theo, a nursery school graduate, was ready to enter kindergarten at the Gateway School in the village, and damned if he didn't need a uniform too.

Roald was euphoric. He hadn't anticipated the mighty thrill it would be to buy a school uniform for Theo until they were well inside the store, picking their way along drab counters piled high with official children's blue and gray. Then, seeing the sartorial Theo gravely eying the goods, the full importance of what it was they were buying struck him with the force of revelation, and he realized in an overwhelming instant that the part of him which hadn't dared count on this day was suddenly set free. Theo needed a uniform. Theo was going to school.

Theo was a bit behind other children his age—how much was difficult to say. His ebullience concealed even the most obvious of his handicaps, the wall-eyed weakness that forced him to cock his head over a coloring book and bear down with the favored eye; it was a drastic angle that his wild eye took, but to observe it, you had to catch him and hold him still. His right hand was useless for writing or drawing and he hadn't yet tamed his left. And sometimes it seemed that his equilibrium was poor, though that was probably plain awkwardness caused by missed years of play. But Theo was bright enough, no question about it, and his will to learn was terrific. He had mastered nearly a hundred flash cards and could spell a few words on his own. That wasn't much evidence to go on, but it was becoming steadily more tempting to imagine that Theo was going to be all right.

"Now don't make Mama look at your things tonight if she's busy," Roald told the children as he backed the Rover into the garage. "I really would suggest that you wait till morning. Tomorrow, she'll want to see everything."

"But, Daddy, what if she asks?" Theo wanted to know, straining to be first into the house.

"If she asks, you show her," Tessa said with a big-sister sigh.

"Yes, Titi, you can show her if she asks," Roald told him, but Theo was already gone.

"When Pat and I met in 1952, we were both eager to get married, but in the abstract," Roald said. I was spending a pleasant evening with Roald, sipping the lees of the dinner wine and enjoying his large small talk. Roald is the best storyteller I know, and listening to him often worked a kind of spell on me. "My being thirty-six, and Pat about ten years younger, it was time for us to get married, and we felt that.

So Lillian Hellman, knowing this and wanting us to meet, invited us to a dinner party, where I behaved badly, I suppose. I was getting into one of those arguments with Lennie Bernstein, and there was no backing off from it. Pat thought I was rude and decided I was 'someone not to know,' as she says. I called her the next day, having got her number from Lillian, and she gave me the brush. I called again and she said she was busy, and again—still busy. But I kept at it, and finally she agreed to see me.

"She was going into the revival of *The Children's Hour* at the time. I had a book that was just coming out, so that left me plenty of time to sit around in the empty theater during rehearsals, and of course I'd nip back to her dressing room as soon as it was over. When the play opened it was pretty much the same routine, my attending a good many performances and clapping wildly, you know, and then afterward we'd go out for supper or to a party with her friends.

"She was in a depressed state when I met her. She was not gay. She was reserved, holding herself in, obviously pretty shaken up all around. She'd come to New York primarily to get away from an unfortunate romance and also to escape the deadening influence of the poor films she was making. I think she planned to work hard as an antidote against her personal misfortunes. So it wasn't a terribly happy girl I was seeing.

"We got married the following July—'53 it would be. A small church wedding, small reception, and then we flew off to Italy. We'd bought a second-hand Jaguar from someone who diddled us and we picked it up in Naples and drove up the Amalfi Drive, then on up through Rome, and on to Geneva and up through the Burgundy country to Paris.

Then we went back to New York; Pat had a play to do or something—*A Roomful of Roses?* No, that was later. This was off-Broadway, a repertory company, very good plays and good roles for Pat.

"Pat moved out of her apartment on Park Avenue and we took a fairly modest place on the West Side. I was writing stories and she was going to classes at the Actors Studio and then appearing in plays at night. She wasn't at all movie-starish; no great closets filled with clothes or anything like that. She had a drive to be a great actress, but it was never as strong as it is with some of these nuts. You could turn it aside. The problem was that you were always up against her coterie of admirers who'd keep telling her, 'Keep working—one right after another.' Actors congregate together, you know. They're not like writers. They huddle and get strength from each other. They were in our apartment all the time, pushing and swarming around, trying to persuade her to keep working, get into some new show. They were all—well, *actors,* and it was me against the lot of them.

"We have absolutely no feeling for this big-Hollywood-salary stuff at all. There's no question that if we'd gone out there and lived as her agent always wanted her to do, and she'd done film after film, she could have worked herself up into a very high bracket. But instead we took to coming back here every summer, and then we bought this little house for four thousand pounds, one little house with a stone-floor kitchen and an old boiler on the side that you washed clothes in."

"Did Pat resist the idea of buying a house in England?" I asked.

"Well, it was done slowly and insidiously by me." Roald

traced circles on the table with a coffee spoon as he talked. At first it was just a little visit. Then we asked to rent a place, and word came back that a nice little place was coming up for sale. She agreed readily enough, and we came and saw it and started putting it right. Obviously it would have been unfair and ridiculous to ask her to spend the winter in this place, so we fell into the routine of being here in summer, back there in winter. It took Pat a little while to get used to country life, but then she seemed to enjoy it and take an interest in things, attending village fetes, crowning Miss Missenden, things like that.

When Roald first met Pat she had deplorable, Hollywood-type furniture throughout her apartment and no eye whatever for paintings or antiques. It still made him wince to remember her horrible satin sofa, an endless beige affair that cost a thousand dollars and eventually grew so tatty that they tried to peddle it to a radio giveaway show, where no one would accept it, even as a prize. But Pat had a great quickness to appreciate things, and in the environment of their marriage she had blossomed in a way that pleased the pedagogue in Roald very much. She grew very rapidly to love good furniture, and soon she knew all the periods and even the woods. She could be fooled, of course, but she wasn't bad—really not bad at all. For years they had bumbled around antique shops in the country, finding bits and pieces for Gipsy House and always aiming for one good piece to take with them and sell when they went to New York; more than once this pleasant fiddle had paid for their round-trip fare.

"For the first seven years of our marriage, we always went to America in the winters purely so she could work on

Broadway or in television. First with one child, then with two, then with three. The only resistance was mine about going back to New York. Gentle resistance, mind you—complaining a bit. But up until Theo's accident, New York was as much our headquarters as Great Missenden. Afterward, though, we didn't want to be there any more. The accident really cooked New York.

"We had a nurse, then, Susan, a good girl, young and cocky. Pat was making *Breakfast at Tiffany's* at the time and I was writing *James*. I was working in Clifford Odets' empty apartment, which was directly above ours. It was December 5, 1960, so Theo was just four months old. Pat was out shopping, and Susan had Theo in his pram, with tiny Tessa walking beside her, on their way to pick up Olivia from her nursery school. They were two blocks from home, at the corner of Eighty-second and Madison. Susan saw the light change, pushed the pram out onto Eighty-second Street, on Madison, and a cab shot past and took the pram right out of her hands.

"Susan dashed across after it. The pram had flown forty feet through the air and into the side of a bus. Tessa was left standing alone on the sidewalk. The police were there within minutes and they rushed them all to the hospital, the four-month-old baby in critical shape, you see, and Tessa and Susan in the back seat of the police car. Pat was a few blocks down the street. She heard the sirens pass but she didn't know what they were for. The telephone was ringing when she got home.

"She called me. 'Theo's been hurt, they say not too seriously. We have to go to Lenox Hill Hospital.' Before I could get out the door Susan called, hysterical, saying hurry, hurry. So then I knew it was bad. Theo was in Emergency when we got there, obviously in bad shape. I called a pediatrician to come in and organize things, and then they took Theo and x-rayed him and found lots of fractures. Very critical shape, they said.

"Pat and I hung around and they began calling in these dreadful special nurses. One creature came in to care for him and the first thing she did was show us a newspaper clipping about the accident and say how thrilled she was to be on the case. Then I saw her giving Theo a dose of some stuff called Dilantin, an anticonvulsant. And she was giving him the most tremendous amount. 'Isn't that rather a lot?' I said. 'No,' she said, 'half an ounce, like it's supposed to be.' Well, it was supposed to be a tenth of a gram, so desperate doctors rushed in and started to stomach-pump him. The poor baby. And while this was going on, the senior neurosurgeon called us in to say he simply wouldn't have all these other doctors in—meaning our pediatrician. It all became very unpleasant. We picked Theo up, wrapped him in blankets and carried him out, with all the doctors standing around looking very worried and protesting.

"It was snowing like hell and we were desperate. But then Harvey Orkin, Pat's agent, suddenly materialized with a car, and he drove very fast and very skillfully through the blizzard, with cars skidding at odd angles all around us. I've not forgotten that ride, because here was Harvey, an unhappyish chap, a wisecracky fellow, someone who in fact was my prime antagonist in these disputes over Pat, a person I wasn't so keen on and who doubtlessly wasn't so fond of me—yet there was Harvey, still the sort of friend who will drive through the snow for you in an emergency. It's easy enough to say anyone would, and much of the time you'd be right. But when it happens, there's not time for people to prove themselves unless they have the instinct for it. There was not a long line of cars waiting at the curbstone—just Harvey's. Harvey had somehow found out, and somehow he knew what was needed.

"At the Presbyterian Hospital, where we took Theo, they operated for a subdural hematoma, which is a kind of swelling caused by bleeding into the brain. They put it right. We took turns staying in his room at the hospital, with one of us going home to try and cheer up Tessa and Olivia. Susan was feeling desperately guilty, and we had her to bring around, too. This went on for about ten days, at the end of which they said we could take him home. He looked groggy, and Pat said right away that she didn't like the looks of him. Then in a day or two he went blind. We took him back and they looked him over and after a couple of hours we were told he had hydrocephalus. 'What's that?' I asked.

"So it was all explained, how the cerebrospinal fluid accumulates around the brain, causing an enlargement of the head and compression of the brain. If the fluid can't be made to escape, the child is finished. The shunt is supposed to carry the fluid off, ideally, down into the right auricle of the heart, which is constantly moving and shaking and in that way keeps the tubing clear, or at least is supposed to. But for us they kept going wrong. The first one only lasted ten days or so before it blocked. Theo went blind and we rushed him in and they operated again. And because he was such a tiny baby, they'd go right in through the fontanelle, push right through to the cortex of the brain, staying out of the motor areas, trying to work in inactive parts, but no doubt doing some damage every time.

"Pat was remarkable during these vigils. She had a kind of strength you could only step back from and admire. In all these terrible moments, she only collapsed once. It was the second time the shunt failed, I think, and she had a mild collapse in the hospital there. She was fed up, she knew they'd cooked him and he wouldn't live long. Because there are only so many places you can put the shunt. Down to the heart through the right jugular vein, then down the left jugular vein, and then they can't use the heart any more and have to start in with the pleura, which usually floods eventually, as it did with Theo, and after that they have to go into all sorts of horrible places like the kidney, which ruins the kidney. And these ghastly operations kept becoming necessary—eight times in less than three years.

"Theo was still going around with the shunt when Olivia died in November '62. Normally we would have been in New York in November. But after the accident we said let's get out of this place where children get hit by taxicabs, and we moved our permanent household here. And of course Olivia wouldn't have died if we'd stayed in New York. They had the inoculations there, but here in England they were not available then. When we were told that Olivia had been in contact with measles, we rang up Ellen, my half sister. Ellen and Louis, who's a commercial artist, were born to my father and his first wife, a Frenchwoman who died when Louis was born. But we all grew up together and feel some of the same family ties. And since Ellen is married to Sir Ashley Miles, the head of the Lister Institute, I asked her if in view of all the trouble we'd had with Theo she could ask

Ashley to provide us with some gamma globulin, just to play it safe with Olivia. The stuff is fairly expensive and scarce. It's always kept on hand for pregnant women who have been in contact with German measles, but it works equally well with measles itself, giving you either temporary immunity or holding it to a very mild case. But Ashley said he couldn't justify breaking the rules for us. It was rotten luck for Ashley and worse luck for us—rotten luck all around, because the odds of contracting encephalitis from measles are very slim, and the odds against a fatal case are roughly ten thousand to one. Our family doctor was not at liberty to call for gamma globulin to protect a child from measles, so when it finally hit her, there we were, stuck out in the country and unprotected.

"On the fifteenth she slept for about twenty-four hours solid, and we didn't like that. I knew she had measles, but I didn't know at the time that there was such a thing as measles encephalitis. I called the doctor, who tested her heart and so on and said that everything would be all right, that it was all just the aftermath of measles. On the morning of the seventeenth she was totally lethargic and drowsy. I tried to play a game with her. I bought a set where you make little animals by twisting pipe cleaners around and I noticed that she couldn't do them at all. But I wasn't excessively worried. I'd taken the doctor's word that this was the aftereffects of measles.

"I was up in my hut at work, and about five o'clock my light flashed twice. Pat had found Olivia unconscious, and when I came in the door she was upstairs shouting down to me that Olivia was having seizures. I dashed up, and she was, and we knew this was a tremendous crisis. We called the doctor and waited, holding her down and trying to stop her from swallowing her tongue. The doctor came. He took one look at her and went deathly pale. We called an ambulance, which arrived in a hurry from the big spine hospital nearby. They came in with their oxygen cylinders and carried her out on a stretcher. I followed in a car. It was about seven in the evening, a Saturday evening. She went straight in and they went to work on her. About ten o'clock I nipped home to see that everything was all right. I stayed about ten minutes, ate a sandwich, then drove right back. When I got there, doctors were prowling around and they looked at me and said, 'You're too late.'

"It happened so swiftly that one didn't have time to prepare for it. I was in a kind of daze, I suppose, and morbid thoughts kept after me. It occurred to me that there must be some tie-up, and that kind of thought can run you down, you know, worrying about fate and the meaning of things. I couldn't do any writing, and that went on for about a year and a half. I had the shunt to work on, because by then Stanley Wade was deep into the problem, and I would go over to his shed and stand around, acting as a sounding-board for his ideas. We were almost through to a solution, and we were hurrying with it, because it still looked like Theo would be wearing one for some time to come, and we had built up a tremendous fear of these operations running on forever, or until they'd just ruined him, you see.

"At the same time, I got the idea that there must be some way of finding out in advance if a child is susceptible to this chance of getting encephalitis from measles. I wanted to set up a careful investigation of this, and I was prepared to get in touch with every parent of every child in this country who had had severe complications from measles. I thought of drawing up a questionnaire and correlating the answers. For example, Olivia had had many smallpox vaccinations but had never built up any antibodies. The things had never taken. She had no reaction at all. So that set me to wondering whether other children who had had measles encephalitis might not have had some similar reaction. So this got started, and a tremendous number of letters went out and a good response came in, turning up a few small, interesting things. But by then the inoculation against measles had become standard in England, so the problem had been very largely erased.

"And very shortly after Olivia died we got a great present, and that was that Theo grew out of his need for the shunt. He went into a bad period of not eating, running a constant slight temperature, looking and acting a little groggy, and he was having fits, too, which were extremely dangerous. So Kenneth Till suggested that we try him without the shunt, going on the premise that perhaps the hydrocephalus had arrested and the shunt itself was causing the trouble. So we agreed and made arrangements for one of us to be at his bed at all times keeping the watch.

"We'd tried it twice before, so we knew what to do. And the signs of danger approaching were very easy to see. He'd vomit and go groggy and they'd race to put in the shunt. Both times we tried it everything was fine for the first five days. Then the symptoms would return. But this time we watched, and the fifth day and then the sixth day came and went. And we didn't dare believe it or count on it too much. And Kenneth said, 'Well, if he goes fifteen days he'll be in the clear.' So we watched and waited, every second, every day, and one by one the fifteen days passed by. And we knew his case had arrested, and that he would live through this thing for sure.

"Pat was better able to cope with the period right after Olivia than I was, I suppose. She never broke down completely and she was always able to talk very freely about it. I think that talking worked for her to help her strengthen herself against the fact of it. Her Southern Protestant upbringing also came to the fore and she became deeply religious—gloom and doom, crime and punishment. She had a very immediate religious feeling that was in many ways like superstition.

"I don't have those feelings at all. I had moments of wondering, of course; and since Pat's aneurysm, especially, I've thought of a tie-up between these misfortunes, all of them striking at the brain. But not in terms of any curse or doom coming down on us, you see—only to think 'How odd.' I don't think I'm capable of taking it beyond that. Superstition is something one grows out of. You try avoiding all the cracks in the pavement or you touch all the posts in the fence. But then you find out later that it doesn't help. You find out that it's not going to make a bit of difference if you step on the cracks or not. I think I just realize subconsciously that if you start thinking about bad luck, you're starting to weaken. The great thing is to keep going, whatever happens.

"But Pat has been stronger, really. A couple of months after the shunt came out, Theo fell from the kissing gate in the garden, and the gate toppled over on him, and he began to lose consciousness. Nothing came of it. He was back to normal very soon. But I tell you, I just froze. I froze in horror, unable to move, while Pat dashed in and called the doctor. I just couldn't see all that work, that brave little boy —everything lost over a garden gate."

Roald rose and walked over to the windows, massaging the small of his back with spread fingers, pushing his long, tired frame into his sway-backed, tiptoed stretch. I got up, imitating him, not knowing what to say. It was two o'clock in the morning.

"There was one thing that had a tremendous influence on me during the war," Roald continued, on the way out the door; it was ritual to end the day with a check of the aviary to make sure that the budgies were sealed in safely from marauding cats. We walked across the lawn, the grass crisp and crackling with early frost. "I imagine you've never heard of 'MacRobert's Reply,' " Roald said. "No? Well, Lady MacRobert was a fine Scottish woman with a manor house, I suppose, and a centuries-old estate—precisely the sort of fossilized old creature you'd probably want to steer clear of. She had three sons, all in the RAF, all pilots, and all of them killed, one after the other, in 1941. I used to know their three names, but now I recall only Alasdair, Sir Alasdair. A lovely name. So Lady MacRobert, upon receiving this news, gave a tremendous sum of money to pay for the cost of a Sterling bomber. And when the plane was built she had painted on it '*Lady MacRobert's Reply*.' I can remember being very moved by that. It was something really dauntless, really indomitable. You simply cannot defeat such people."

As always, the budgies were safe behind the screens, sleeping in absolute silence, beaks buried under wings. We turned back toward the house. "Splendid sky tonight," Roald said, looking up past the black-on-black horizon. "Have you read much Lawrence? Somewhere he says: 'The stars were *snapping* in the sky.' Doesn't that tell it beautifully? That one perfect word is enough, I should think, to place Lawrence firmly among the immortals."

❂

Pat's vanity returned in full bloom from its half year of neglect, and for the first time since the stroke she brushed her hair and put on lipstick, smiled into mirrors, asked everyone how she looked. But that alone did not account for the dimension of the change that had come over her, nor did the bloom of maternity still in her cheeks. It was something more vital, like the end of an illness—and it was tempting to believe that her illness was really at its end. There were still indications in her speech and movements of damage that had yet to heal, but the promise of healing seemed unmistakable. In the months I had spent visiting Gipsy House, I was always made uneasy by Roald's talk of a "hundred percent recovery." Now Pat's cheerful radiance seemed to bear him out miraculously, and his optimism became infectious: everyone agreed that the change in Pat after only six months made any recovery possible in the end.

Pat was full of the kind of active good will that no one really ill can manage. She was still awkward with the children and around the house, but she stopped becoming discouraged before trying. She had little patience with herself, but there was much less anger and, it seemed, much less fear. Talking with her ceased to be the mental and moral exercise it had been a few months before. She liked herself better, and when she spoke of her past it was clear that she didn't suffer the memory.

"I know who I was in that film. I could tell you about her

. . . only I can't think of her name. Alma! I was Alma, that's right, and I'm very sorry to have to tell you that I was a good Alma, a very fine Alma. She wasn't married, but she'd been married. She was no *longah* a virgin. But I can't tell you any more about her, except that she lives in this house . . . She's the only one there who lives in this house, the only woman, all the others are . . . husbands. Their wives have died, though, so they have Alma, to . . . take care of the house. Except the little one—there's a boy . . . ohhhh, sixteen, a young boy—he doesn't have a wife. I mean he didn't . . . Oh, Jesus! How do you tell a story? *The little one was too young.* Just the old one, his . . . grandfather, had a wife, but the wife was dead, and he had this farm, a big farm for cattle—ranch! It was a ranch, and his son, who was Hud, was there, and his grandson and Alma. And the father, the old one, he died, and Hud, he tried to rape me, I'm very sorry to tell you, and I didn't like that so I left. And it was a beautiful picture.

"Then there were some others I liked. One was where I fell in love with a kind of cowboy singer. It begins in a radio station, I think, my part does, and he has come to sing on the radio. Is that it? *Face in the Crowd,* that was it! Have you seen the scarecrow up by the raspberries? His head is that man, the leading man. They had dolls made of him to—you know, help the picture . . . promote it!—and that scarecrow has the head of one of those dolls. But it was a good picture, with a gr-r-reat di-rector—Elia Kazan! Isn't his name . . . *Gadge?* I think they call him Gadge, I know they do. And he's a gr-r-reat man. So that was good. I liked that one. It was the first good one I made. And then there was . . . *one other one,* a good one, mind you—but I've forgotten what one it was. *Breaking Point?* I was trying to have an affair with the husband? He was somebody's husband, and I was a rotten woman to have done it, heh, heh, heh. We went out on a boat. The leading man had a boat, he was the captain. That's how I met him, because I was with somebody else, and we took this boat together, and the leading man—*John* Garfield!—he was the captain of the boat we took. And I think he hated us at first, but then afterward he loved me. And the police were coming after him, I think, but I forget why . . . And after that I forget the rest of it . . .

"The thing was, I began too easily. Everything I did at first was something . . . you'd forget. The things I did in California weren't good. I couldn't do anything good when I was there. But then when I came back to New York I seemed to be able to act a lot. I always wanted to be good, mind you, but that doesn't mean I could do it.

"But I'm very sorry to tell you that it meant a whole lot to me. I wanted to be a gr-r-reat actress. I couldn't give it up and I knew it. But *now* I'm going to give it up, baby. I'm forced to. I'll never act again because I can't remember lines. This is the *first time* in my life that I don't feel like an artist. I mean it. I always felt like one before, and of course I used to be. An artist, a gr-r-reat, gr-r-reat actress, heh, heh, heh. Now Papa is the only artist. I'll always think of *him* as an artist, because he is, you know. Have you read his books? *Great books!* Of course I wouldn't understand *one word* now. I used to, though. Papa used to love to have me read his stories. I'm very sorry to tell you that he used to . . . bring them to me. He would. He'd bring them, and he'd say, 'Tell me what you think.' And I would, I really would. And sometimes I even said, 'Well, wel-l-ll, what about this?'

Sometimes he took my advice, too. But sometimes he'd say, 'God, Pat!' and get very, very cross with me. Not really. He's a great man and I love him.

"I love *everybody*. Lucy and Ophelia and Tessa and Theo and Papa and you and Asta and . . . Alfhild! and . . . Else! and Nicky and Anna and Louise and . . . Jenny and Sarah. No! Not Sarah. I do not like her one bit. Except I really do, you know. I'm not even cross with her. There are people I'm cross with, but I can't think of anybody. I can't think of *one person* who's made me cross. I'm starting from scratch again . . ."

In all the time since the stroke, Pat's only public outing had been a visit to Games Day at Tessa's school, where she sat on the grass with the other parents and watched the girls compete for "The Olivia," a tall, shining trophy Pat had won for something or other years before and had given to the school in memory of her daughter's grace and skill at games. It had not been a happy afternoon. Tessa won no prizes and Pat became morose thinking of Olivia. Family excursions and evenings out were unpredictable, and Roald did not encourage them.

But now Pat felt ready for a night or two out. That seemed a good sign, so Roald took her out to supper several times in the space of a week or two, and she thrived on it. She had acquired a delightful, ingenuous way with waiters and with diners at adjoining tables. "Is it good what you're eating?" she would ask, and her manner was such that people would always tell her. A few weeks later, when she said she would like to see a movie, Roald made the mistake of taking her to *Help!*, the Beatles' adventuresome nonsense film. She sat through the ninety minutes shaking her head in dismay and whispering that she couldn't understand what it was all about; and Roald tried in vain to convince her that you weren't supposed to.

A month or so after Lucy's arrival, Pat's friends held a dinner in her honor at her favorite restaurant, a gourmet's pub called The Bell in Aston-Clinton, a village fifteen minutes from Great Missenden. Vidal Sassoon sent his best hairdresser up from London to cut Pat's wispy hair, and she arrived at the dinner looking lovely and transformed. She sat between The Hawk and Marty Ritt, and in the toasts that followed the long, happy meal, one praised her art and the other her great strength and capacity for life. It was a tender and emotional evening in which the testimonials revealed the sense of wonderment everyone felt at Pat's recovery. Then Pat herself rose and proposed a toast "to you . . . my good, good friends."

The dinner seemed to mark an end to the deepest worries for Pat's future, and indeed it was true that things were returning to normal. Roald was finding a little time for writing again and Pat was busy with her lessons. Her eye patch, curled and torn, was at the bottom of Tessa's toy chest, and the leg brace was hanging on a peg in the hallway, like someone's forgotten umbrella. Pat was still apologetic and sometimes depressed, but she talked and laughed like a person with hopes for the future. She even confided to Roald that in recent days she had begun to detect certain stirrings of her old belief in God. "You see how it works?" he said. "With no prodding at all from me or the vicar, the devil is losing his grip on you."

7

THE FIRST six months following a stroke are generally considered the period in which the patient may expect to make his greatest gains, and in Pat's case this was true. Six months after her stroke she had overcome all the drastic impairments it had left upon her. But in another sense, it was only then that her true rehabilitation began—not the work of recovery that made her a functioning person again, but the subtler, longer lessons that made her into the person she used to be, or someone very much like her. Only after Lucy's birth, after Gipsy House got off its invalid's footing and Roald began to turn his attention away from the crisis of her illness—only then did Pat begin the long march that finally brought her home.

It was an undramatic time of slow progress that followed the early miracles and the leveling, reinvolving event of Lucy's birth; for Pat, it was in many ways a terrible, dreary time, the most boring and unrewarding of all. Her mind and body continued to seek very little beyond a kind of comfort that led to withdrawal, and it was only by working steadily against the grain of her desires that she advanced toward her cure. It was grit—abetted by Roald's cajolery—that gave her the will to keep at it, since she herself could detect no change from one month to the next.

Throughout the autumn and winter, there was so much mail coming in for her that Roald could not keep up composing the careful answers he felt these letters deserved. In the first eighteen months after her stroke, Pat never received less than a hundred letters a week, most of them asking advice, as if she had become an authority on strokes and their long, arduous rehabilitation. Pat would sort the mail in the morning, gloating happily over how much more there was for her than for Roald. Sometimes letters reached her with addresses like "Actress Patricia Neal, England" and "Mrs. Roald Dahl (Pat Neal), Village of Grate Missington." She laughed with delight at every letter marked "Ronald" or "Mr. and Mrs. Patricia Neal," putting them aside so Roald would be sure to notice. Letters that came from family and friends she often answered herself, typing out her replies left-handed and in capital letters on her new electric typewriter; the rest was left to Roald, who always wrote by hand.

The letter writers took their cue from newspapers and magazines, which had begun to picture Pat as close to fully recovered. In January 1966, less than a year after the press had stood its long vigil for her, a spate of stories from Hollywood reported that Mike Nichols had offered her a leading role in *The Graduate* ("By September I'm sure she'll be ready to go back to work," Roald was quoted as saying).

When September came, Pat was by no means ready, but the letters continued, congratulating her and asking for the secret of her cure.

Roald was intensely proud of the progress she had made and he was convinced that she owed it completely to hard work. They had evolved a good technique of rehabilitation and he wanted to share it with the despairing people who looked to her as a fount of optimism. So he had a long and careful letter mimeographed, and sent it out to whoever seemed to be lost in the trackless mystery of the illness:

> A stroke patient who is having difficulty with speech, writing, reading, memory or concentration, and who suffers inevitably from inertia, boredom, frustration and depression, can be helped enormously by amateurs in his or her own home.
>
> The person upon whom the patient is dependent, be it husband, wife, father, mother, brother, sister or best friend, should never, in my opinion, take on the onerous duty of rehabilitation. That person should reserve his or her energies for running the house or earning a living, and above all, keeping cheerful.
>
> So the first thing to do is to make a list of all one's closest friends who live within visiting distance. These will be mainly female—wives whose husbands are at work. About ten is a good number, but even three or four is a help. Then phone them all up and ask if they can give a couple of hours a week or four hours a week, or best of all, an hour a day. Then draw up a roster, so that the first friend (who is now a "teacher") arrives not later than 10 A.M. (9 A.M. is better). The next arrives an hour later to take over, and so on right through the day until 6 P.M., with a two- or three-hour break for lunch and rest.
>
> The friends will protest at first, saying they know nothing about how to teach people suffering from aphasia, etc. To this

you reply that they don't have to know anything. The whole thing is common sense. All the patient wants is practice.

Patricia Neal was given precisely this treatment from the very first week she arrived home in England. (The earlier you start, the greater the chance of recovery.) Her first teacher arrived at 9 A.M. The last one left at 6 P.M. She had three hours off at lunchtime. And they made her work very hard. But they also taught her to play dominoes and other games in between. Recreation and fun is an important part of the programme.

In order to give some guidance and confidence to prospective teachers, Pat's teachers have drawn up a very brief summary of what they did and how they went about it. This is enclosed. All prospective teachers will profit by reading it. And I may say that at the end of six months, none of Pat's teachers were amateurs any longer. They were pros. They had become extraordinarily skillful. They had also enjoyed their work, and I would back them now to take on almost any case (which is not *too* severe) and show the patient how to live.

ROALD DAHL

With the letter was enclosed a five-page outline headed "Notes by Pat's Teachers":

The fields where the amateur can help particularly are:

1) Trouble with speech and in the comprehension of words in all their forms.

2) Difficulty in thinking out or solving even the simplest of problems.

3) Lack of confidence in general—teach them that everything learnt throughout their lives is still available to them.

4) Extreme inertia and lack of concentration.

So, to deal with them one by one:

1) *Words*

a) Read young children's books with the patient. Use the pictures these little books always have to help the story along. Allow gestures, stumbles and half-words, *any* means of communication and "getting places."

b) Take any simple word—say, "black"—and get the patient to say it, put it into a sentence, find the opposite word, a word that rhymes with it, explain what it means. Then look it up in the dictionary together (always allowing the patient to do the thumbing through, helping only where necessary).

c) Get the patient to tell stories and describe things using such words as he can manage, gestures, pictures drawn by him or got out of a book. Let the patient stew over getting himself across. If he uses gestures, etc., then the teacher can supply the words for him. Try to get the patient to repeat them.

d) Lay objects out on a tray and get the patient to identify them, then to memorize them.

e) Make up very simple crosswords for the patient. Let him have a dictionary always by him. Maybe he will remember the first letter of the word he seeks; he will then have a chance of finding it on his own. (Let him do the work wherever possible, teacher doing the stimulating, pushing, vitalizing side of the partnership.)

f) Later, get on to reading well-written sentences, paragraphs, half-pages, and explaining what he has just read. Also, do all the above to a higher standard.

Warning: Don't treat the patient as a child.

2) *Thinking Out, Solving Problems*

a) Do jigsaws (cut up the pictures from magazines yourself to begin with, then get on to children's jigsaws, then adults').

b) Write out an easy sentence, cut it up word by word, and let the patient put the sentence together again.

c) Do simple arithmetic. Try it aurally—mental arithmetic.

d) Play simple games like dominoes, card games, ludo, even scrabble. Get the patient to identify shapes—in card games, hearts from diamonds—geometric shapes, silhouettes.

e) Play "I Spy" on a wet day. On a car journey, make up names to fit license plates (e.g., GLP could be "Gallop").

f) Invent your own games to produce mental stimulus, suiting them to the condition of the patient. Concentration is what you're after. Concentration and recall.

3) *Confidence in Themselves and Their Knowledge*

a) Try to talk about every imaginable subject, no holds barred, no scruples, no "unmentionables."

b) Go through the encyclopedia with him. Watch reactions carefully and stress subjects where interest is plain. Also tackle anything from which the patient appears to run away.

c) Go through any book of information—painters, cricket scores, music, newspapers—wherever interest lies.

d) Get him to observe things—furniture, sunset, birds, cooking, garden.

4) *Inertia, Bad Concentration*

a) Quick, easy questions banged at the patient like a machine gun (you'll need a million of these). Answer by words, gestures, pointing, miming, anyhow.

b) Push, push, push for answers, make the patient sit up, try like mad, dig out something from somewhere, mangle out a bit of vitality, a laugh, an *effort*.

5) *Oddments*

a) Remember that memory is attached to *picturing* things. (Pat still doesn't do this to an average extent).

b) Teacher must attempt to be: encouraging
nonemotional
gay
firm
never talk down

c) Keep the patient out of the way of undue STRESS (however trivial or awkward-making the cause appears to be). *Bother about this.* Do *not* shield him from the general run of "woes," separate this carefully from real stress. To be emotional is okay, to be irritated beyond your control is not.

❂

Sarah had submitted her name to a marriage bureau before the autumn of 1965 was out, and she hit it off happily with the second man they sent around, a soldier who took her off to Germany. Jenny left a few months later, love-struck for a fitter in the RAF, and soon she was sending back post cards mailed from Singapore. Gipsy House was less inclined to intervals of teen-age hysteria with the two girls gone, but there was no question about replacing them immediately. Roald had just got into a routine of work in his writing hut, but he dropped everything to conduct another talent search.

First he hired Klara, a solid young Hungarian girl who spoke and smiled in such a charming way that prudent Roald signed her up to be the children's nurse on the basis of taking her along on a shopping trip to Amersham one day. Then he found Rita, a pretty Italian teen-ager whose English was less serviceable than Klara's, but who spoke just as effectively in the benevolent language of the eyes. She came from a Catholic orphanage near Naples which Roald and Marjorie Clipstone, as chairman and secretary of the Missenden Branch of International Help for Children, had been supporting for several years. Pat and the children liked the new girls right away, and Roald admitted after just a few months' observation that they seemed remarkably sensible and settled for "young heifers."

Roald wrote a screenplay that winter, for *You Only Live Twice,* the last of the big James Bond epics. It was the first time in his life that he turned out something not specifically original, although the novel was so fragmentary that his script had to draw heavily on his own well of invention—which produced a volcano missile bunker, Pentagon War Room scenes and a host of other departures from the text that seemed to fit the classic Bond design. Roald's taste for adventuring made the work tolerable; he found fun and excitement in consorting with his Midas-like producers, Albert "Cubby" Broccoli and Harry Saltzman, flying round-trip to Los Angeles as though it were nothing, staying in Howard Hughes's cottage at the Beverly Hills Hotel, having Irving "Swifty" Lazar for an agent. On occasion, he even sent his manuscripts down to London by chauffeur-driven Rolls. And then, of course, there was the true reward—an astounding lot of money.

Roald had renounced the theater forever, thirteen years before, after making a disastrous Broadway debut with a play called *The Honeys*. The many embarrassments of *The Honeys* were etched deeply in his memory, and though he could speak lightly of it now, he left little doubt that the experience had soured him on writing grist for other people's mills.

With *The Honeys* behind him and Pat's career developing nicely, he went for years without feeling the slightest temptation to go after the kind of money that the stage and movies might bring. His tastes as well as Pat's were fully satisfied by their two moderate incomes, and they had only worked on what they themselves wanted, watching opportunities go by. They bought no stocks or shares, not even insurance, operating on the premise that if anything happened to either of them, the other could always earn a living—not a very wise premise, as Roald now admitted. He was almost fifty, and though he felt in far better health than at thirty or forty, it was still unsettling to consider how old he would be before the children were grown. And much as he resisted allowing the idea to take hold in his mind or be hinted at in anyone's conversation, it was still quite possible that Pat would never work again. A heart attack would leave Pat and the children with the house, the paintings and his royalties—something, but not enough to die on.

He had sold his first original screenplay, *Oh Death Where Is Thy Sting-a-ling-a-ling?*, in the month after Pat's stroke, but in his urgency had settled for half the money agreed upon, and the unpleasantness of that experience only confirmed his aversion to any dealings involving producers and directors. But when Cubby Broccoli called to offer him the Bond film, he was caught at his moment of maximum financial worry, and he quickly accepted with a great and liberating sense of new security—more money rolling in immediately than years of crafting stories could bring.

The transition was easy; it was far less difficult to write the screenplay than short stories. Roald ran through the assignment respecting his deadlines, "conferencing" with the silk-suited tribe of production men, performing in all respects like an old studio regular. Pat was delighted to witness Roald, in his deerstalker and ankle-length, twenty-year-old tweed overcoat, striking out for London in the morning to meet with "Cubby & Co.," as he called his associates, all of whom were manicured, white-on-white necktied, cigar-loving handsome tippers. It was marvelous and bizarre that

Roald, of all people, should fit so snugly into this aerie of high-priced eagles; in everything but his wardrobe, he seemed to have made an effortless transition from elegantly shabby country Englishman to a high-priced Hollywood screen writer whose occasional story appeared in *Playboy*. Pat pretended to be jealous whenever the overseas operator asked for Roald or when lavish gifts for the children were delivered to the house by moguls courting Roald instead of her. Or perhaps jealousy was what she really felt, her pride and enthusiasm being the pretense. "I think that Roald is a genius, a great man, and I'm sincerely happy that he's earning a living" was what she said. And usually she added that now she wouldn't have to work again herself.

The movie was shot on location in Japan, and in the late summer of 1966 Roald took Pat with him to stay for the first two weeks of the month he would be there. He had imagined that the trip would be a great treat for her, giving her a holiday from her lessons and enlarging the horizon that had tightened around her from such a long stay at home. But Pat lacked the energy for much tourism and she returned from the trip with only the vaguest impression of the country she had seen. The stroke was well over a year behind her, but it was still too early for some things.

The souvenirs that Roald brought home from Japan could well have been the loot of a regiment. There were large, rubber-faced dolls who sang shrill Japanese lullabies for Lucy and Ophelia; FM-AM shortwave walkie-talkies for Tessa and Theo; a miniature television set; a pocket-size metal hand warmer; a pair of binoculars; a battery-powered sonar beacon guaranteed to mesmerize lake fish into perfect submission for Alex, Asta's hearty husband, who, being a Scotsman and a veterinarian, gasped at the ungodly genius behind this undreamed-of lure. There were pearls for Pat; a wall clock in the form of a giant wrist watch with a four-foot alligator strap; paper fans and umbrellas; tiny rickshaws of balsa and bamboo; plastic-ivory geisha dolls; toy helicopters; satchels full of fantastic Japanese gimmicks—a present or two or three for everyone who was there.

Pat, like the children, was delirious. "Papa! My God! Where did you get time for all this shopping?" she asked between choruses of "Ooohhh!" The sisters and their families were more restrained, as if dismayed at the prodigious unbundling of surprise that was making their own gifts for Roald shrink steadily in comparison to his amazing gifts for them. It was September 13, 1966, and they had come over to celebrate Roald's fiftieth birthday.

Pat was in splendid form. The apologetic Pat of the summer before had vanished and in her place sat a woman not only younger and stronger but also louder and more aggressive—even bigger, it seemed. I had always felt a little sorry for her at family gatherings; the Dahls were so big and so healthy that a roomful of them was intimidating, almost stifling, as though their broad tweedy shoulders and abundance of blond hair somehow took the oxygen out of the air, making Pat appear wan and withdrawn, the smallest person in the room. But now her laughter was full of raucous whoops and hoots and her resonant voice could easily be heard over the babble of twenty adults and children. "*Roooo*ald!" she hollered, rolling it out with a Sophie Tucker rasp. "*Roooo*ald, can I have another martini? 'N,' baby, you *better* say yes." She was having a whale of a time, and everybody knew it.

Roald's sisters thought that the two weeks Pat had spent running the house while Roald was away explained the latest advance in her recovery.

"She did jolly well here by herself," Else told Roald. Else had looked in on Pat every day, but Rita and Klara seemed to be all the help she needed. "I think some time away from you was the best thing in the world for her."

Everyone agreed. Roald was so omnipresent and dependable that a week or two without him was like throwing away the leg brace.

The party swirled through the house with the children underfoot, launching the helicopter, lying down behind the two long sofas to secretly broadcast their walkie-talkie giggles, pulling the wind-up cords that set the dolls to piping. Roald and the brothers-in-law exchanged awed words of praise for the ingenuity of the Japanese; as veterans of the RAF (John and Roald) and the Battle of Britain (Alex and Alfhild's husband, Leslie) they could never speak this way of the hated Germans, but the Japanese, as they kept saying, were damned admirable, no matter what you said about them.

I was talking to Klara and Rita in the kitchen when Pat came in and gathered them both into her arms. "What I love about these two beautiful girls," she said, "is that they don't speak any better than I do—*do* you," and with that her hug became two tickling hands that sent them both spinning.

"Pat is in fantastic form," I told Roald the first time we had a moment alone.

"I'm afraid she's had too much to drink," he said. "The

injured brain simply cannot stand alcohol. The effect can be devastating."

"Roald. Are you talking about me?" It was Pat at the kitchen door, flooding the room with a stage glower.

"I was just telling Barry here that you've had too much to drink."

"I have not! Don't you say that!"

"Ah, but you have, Pat."

"Roald! You're a rotten man for saying that! She came across the room in an elaborate, operatic attack, slapping at his shoulders with her strong left hand.

"You be the judge," Roald said to me from behind defending arms.

Pat turned away from Roald to face me down in the same half-clowning way: "You better watch what you say, baby."

I grinned at them, hoping to convey loving neutrality. "I'd say . . . I don't know—a bit much? How's that?"

Pat was on me in a flash, playfully thrashing my back, hitting harder than I knew she could. "Ooooo, you're as rotten as he is. You're evil, the two of you." Her face collapsed, melted into tears, and without another word she was gone, limping away sharply in her best effort to stomp, turning quickly up the stairs to the bedroom. Roald watched her go. "I don't like ticking her off like that," he said, "but alcohol is the worst thing in the world for her."

"I haven't had a single dream since this thing happened to me," Pat remarked as we sat down to dinner one night. "Not *one dream.* I guess I just don't have a brain left to dream with." She wrinkled her nose and laughed briefly to herself, then took another swallow of wine. Roald was twisting a corkscrew into a fresh bottle of Beaujolais and didn't appear to be listening. He usually had ample wine uncorked in time to let it breathe for an hour before dinner, but on this night he had slipped up. The children were already finishing their supper and they listened impassively, as though they had heard about dreams before or could not be made to think about dreaming.

"What can you do to make yourself dream?" Pat asked the table at large. "It's sad not to dream. I would sincerely like to have some dreams again."

"You cannot *try* to dream," Klara asserted.

"Maybe that's why I'm so crazy," Pat said, laughing more fully. "Roald says he's going to send me to the nutty home or something."

"What?" Tessa said, looking up with sudden interest.

"Your mother was making a joke, Teddy," Roald explained. "Who would like wine?"

"Roald, you are not telling the truth," Pat said evenly, fixing him with a combative eye. "You told me that I was heading for the nutty home."

"No, Pat. I never said that. What I actually said was that you were becoming a comic figure—"

"Like someone in the nutty home . . ."

"Hardly, Pat. I wouldn't have said that."

Pat jumped to her feet and raised her glass high above her head. "I would like to propose a toast to Roald," she said. "To Roald, a great man, a great father and husband, a great, gr-reat writer—"

"And the best bridge player in Buckinghamshire," Roald interjected.

"—and the best bridge player in Buckinghamshire," Pat added, soaking the phrase in sarcasm. Pat drank and the others complied with the toast, clicking glasses and smiling around the table.

"This is Pat's new number," Roald told me. "How many toasts have you heard in the past week?"

"About ten."

"Oh, no!" Pat protested.

"You've missed about ten thousand toasts, I'm afraid," Roald said. "She'll drink a toast to anyone or anything."

"I'll drink to that!" Pat exclaimed, collapsing into laughter.

"You'd better mind your manners next week when you go up to London for the Woman of the Year luncheon," Roald said. "You don't want to be climbing up on your chair to drink toasts when you've got all those powerful females around taking notes on you. You're being honored as one of the lionesses of the British Empire. All the great Dames will be there."

"And I'm going alone on the train . . ."

"Yes, she's made up her mind to make the trip alone. It will be her first solo since the aneurysm."

"Terrific, Pat," I said.

"And did you tell him about the dinner in New York for the mental people?" she asked Roald.

"Ah, yes—Pat is to be the featured speaker at a dinner at the Waldorf next February for the benefit of brain-injured children. All the big moguls will be there, looking her over, you see—"

"—and all my friends are coming," Pat said.

"Yes, it will be a gala evening and Pat has undertaken to give a speech."

"Ho, ho, ho! I didn't have anything to do with it. *He signed me up.*"

"Technically, that's correct, but you want to do it."

"I don't want to do it. I don't want to have anything to do with it."

"Wait until the photographers start clustering around and the *New York Times* calls for an interview. You'll be ecstatic."

"Yeah."

When it was time to tuck the children in bed, Pat went up with them and was gone for nearly half an hour. When she came down again there was something about her that spoke of accomplishment, the flush in her cheeks, the way she tossed back a falling lock of hair.

"Pat's got the bedtime technique down cold again," Roald remarked. "Six months ago she couldn't have done that."

"Do you think so?" Pat asked. Her tone betrayed the unmixed pleasure she felt whenever he spoke of the progress she had made.

"Oh, listen, six months ago it was a fight to get you up there in the first place, and then you'd make a cock of it. Something would frustrate you or make you angry and you'd come storming down with the nippers all screaming in their beds."

"*Roald,*" Pat purred. "That's not right." She wasn't taking him seriously.

But Roald persisted. "I mean it. You're unaware of the marvelous improvement over the last year or six months because to you it goes so slowly. But you were really quite incapable of simply getting along with the children and making them feel comfortable around you. Now, if you'll only take it a little further and play marvelous games with them like you used to, and sing and tell them stories—"

"But I do!" She was back on the defensive now.

"Only when really pressed, Pat. You've got to admit it. Now and then you'll make a small effort, but it's not the natural, flowing response it has to be."

"Well, listen, you don't know how many complaints—"

"What complaints?" Roald asked. He had gone into the kitchen and was spooning preserved raspberries into a large glass bowl.

"Com*plaints*. From Theo. There were a lot of complaints at first but now there aren't and he gets a good night's sleep when I put him to bed now."

A triumphant, knowing look settled upon Roald. "Aha. And why is that?"

"Because I was a very good lady. I per-ser-vered. And I've *loved* birth. I'm very good at birthing babies." Pat chuckled to herself and smiled around the table. Roald brought in the bowl of raspberries and placed it at the center of the table. Rita laid out large silver spoons and glass dishes; Klara mixed the instant coffee. Roald went back to the kitchen and returned with a bread box full of candy bars, and Pat poured a glass of wine. "Pat, you've got raspberries and coffee and you don't need wine," he said.

Pat leaped up from her chair to get within punching range of Roald. "*RRRRrrrruh!*" She pounded his shoulder with the heel of her hand, then burst into happy laughter. "Oh, Papa, you're right, I know you are."

"Now, let's change the subject—"

"I don't want to change the subject," Pat said. "Just tell me what I'm doing wrong and what you want me to do."

It was hard to make out from Pat's manner if she was genuinely asking for criticism and advice or simply spoiling for more mock combat. She was still smiling, but she also seemed chastened; she rocked back and forth between flashes of defiance and abrupt little sprays of laughter. Roald tilted his head back, pursed his lips and brought his fingertips together at a point just below his chin, where he held them like the scales of justice. Finally he peered out over the temple of his hands and said quietly, "First, be cheerful. Second, be helpful. Third, stop sitting around on your butt in the mornings."

Pat was out of her chair and down the table flailing at him before the words were out of his mouth. "Oh, Roald, you make me so angry," she said. "You act like I don't do anything around here."

"Well . . ."

"Look, Roald, I'm Southern—and it's just coming out now."

Everyone laughed merrily at this, Pat's laughter running a half beat behind the rest, as though she hadn't counted on such good response. Then all went to work on the raspberries, eating in silence until Roald said, "Do you realize that Olivia picked these berries down by the hedge five or six years ago?" Pat looked up and after a moment she and Roald exchanged grave smiles. Then they went back to their eating, spooning up the red raspberry liquor until the last drops were gone.

✿

Pat and I prowled through the cluster of shops at the approach to High Street—the dairy, the little supermarket, the greengrocer's at the corner—shops that Pat visited nearly every day. She was without question the easiest mark in Great Missenden, and the merchants all loved to see her coming. She would limp in the door in her bright-green coat and tall baby-blue boots, brow furrowed in study of the shopping list she held creased and twisted in her hands. She always composed the list carefully with Rita's help, but it served only as the barest outline for her inspired shopping—above and beyond it, there was much worth buying, and she never returned to the house without some frozen chocolate soufflés or imported cocktail crackers or taco mix or smoked minced oysters. She would pass her packages on to Mr. Lambert, a tall, gaunt North Countryman who had recently been added to the changing staff of Gipsy House as yardsman, handyman and chauffeur. Mr. Lambert always put on a dark coat and driver's cap for these outings, and helped Pat by carrying the cornucopic boxes of groceries out to the Triumph. Then he would get into the car and follow Pat along the three-hundred-yard-long High Street, finally picking her up at the butcher's for the half-mile ride up the lane.

"I'm so happy that you think I'm bet*tah*," Pat said to me over her shoulder. She was sniffing through the cheeses in the dairy. "But there's still plenty that's wrong. The fact that I can't learn lines. I think I could act if I could remember lines. I think so, but I don't know. I'm probably wrong. And then I limp. And my head goes in, which I don't like a bit. It goes in over here on the left side, you see." She ran her finger across her temple, tracing the slight depression above her cheekbone; I had noticed it long before, but somehow I was surprised that Pat was aware of it, especially now that it had become very subtle.

"And then my hand doesn't work right. I write like a kid. I can light a cigarette, though, and I think I smoke with my right hand. I probably don't, though. I probably use my left. I know I should use my right all the time, but I'm sick and tired of exercising. I just don't want to exercise any more. I don't think the exercises help at all. It's just living from day to day that helps you."

We headed down High Street, stopping in at the drugstore, the gift shop and the post office, as well as the town's other bakery, where Pat bought buns for tea. Apart from Mrs. Thurgar, the druggist's wife, the shopkeepers did not pay her special attention—either out of diffidence or merely because they were a breed of shopkeepers as frugal with sentiment as with money. But Pat still dealt with them in her lavish, rococo style.

"Would you care to have this wrapped?"

"I would sincerely appreciate it."

"How about some bacon to go with the kidney?"

"A *splendid* idea, and I thank you *for it.*"

We stopped to examine the window display at the bookstore. "It's a rotten thing, but they don't have all of Roald's books here," Pat said. "They are meant to have all his books in piles in the window so that everybody will know that he lives in the village." The bearded owner waved pallidly from inside the window and Pat shook her fist at him. "*Rrrrr!* Get those books," she shouted through the glass.

"I love wearing these boots because they *stay on,*" she said as we crossed the street to the waiting Lambert. "When I try to wear shoes, the right one keeps flapping and slipping off and I can't do what you have to do with your toes to keep it on. Curl or squeeze your toes, whatever it is you do." I dropped back a pace to observe Pat's walk; it was so much better than before that I had scarcely been conscious of the limp that persisted, a stiffness in her right leg which made her swing it forward in a slight arc, as though it were longer than the left; at the curbstone she came to a full stop before lifting the right foot up and planting it down on the sidewalk.

Pat was amazed at the abundance of things she had bought, once we were home and the packages were spread on the table. Apart from asparagus tips, bisquits, canned nuts from America, sample pounds of unknown brands of Dutch and Danish butter and a set of comic tea towels, her purchases were as sound and sensible as a mess sergeant's: six large jars of instant coffee, a dozen cans of cleansing powder, twenty-five pounds of meat. Lambert carried these staples down the steps to the basement, which was lined with heavy shelves stockpiled with provisions, and where there was also a large gleaming freezer and a stretch of wall set up with bins and brick dividers for storing of wine; it could have been the pantry of a small hotel.

"It's marvelous to go shopping now that Roald's so rich," Pat said with a sprinkle of laughter. "Do you know that he made more money writing that one film than I ever made in my career? Although I won the Oscar. It makes me very angry to think they like him so much more than me." She laughed again. "Of course Roald's a genius, he really is, and they're very lucky to have him working on their films. And now that he's making so much money, I won't have to make any more films, which is good because I can't act, anyhow. I can't remember lines." She laughed, and when I didn't join her she grabbed my wrist and squeezed it until I laughed too.

"Is Patricia at home?" The caller looked like a fat and powerful Dylan Thomas, but he spoke in a little mouse voice. "She won't remember me. Tell her I'm the porcelain dealer from Brill who always worshiped her."

"Tell him to come in!" Pat shouted. She was listening from her perch at the kitchen table, where she was settled over her afternoon coffee.

He came into the room almost on tiptoe, seeming to retreat a half step with every pace forward. "Patricia, you won't remember me . . ."

"Oh, yes, I do," Pat said in a voice both stronger and deeper. "You're the one who has that shop. And we bought some—ah, glasses? Or dishes?"

"Yes, yes, yes," the dealer murmured, easing himself slowly into a chair, as if in fear that someone would notice that he was sitting down. "I was just driving through the village, Patricia, and I thought I would just drop by for a moment and pay my respects to you. It's been six years, you know, and I've read so much about you . . ."

"Has it been *six years?*" Pat thundered back at him. It appeared that she assumed from his whisper that his hearing was poor.

"Yes, yes, Patricia, it has, it has. I'll just stay a minute—"

"No! No! Would you like a cup of coffee?"

"Well, yesss . . ."

"Good. You're a very good man to stay." The dealer was

disconcerted by the warmth of her reception; he kept his eyes fixed on his lap while Pat curled forward in her chair the better to see him, her eyes alight at this unexpected face from the past.

"But you were closed!" she suddenly said, remembering. They had driven past his shop one day, meaning to stop, but the place was empty, out of business. "Didn't you go out of business?"

"Well, yes, Patricia, I've had my troubles, just as you have . . ."

"Really? What happened?"

"Oh, it's a long story, but basically, I was put into hospital for a time, you see, and I had to start all over."

"What do you mean 'put in'? Do you mean the nutty home?"

"Well, yes, in fact, it was."

"My God! What for? Did you really go dotty?"

The dealer squirmed in his chair, smiling miserably around at the eavesdropping household; even Theo had dropped everything to listen in. "Well, it was my wife, you see. She thought so, and she was able to persuade others, and it was done."

"That's amazing," said Pat, straining to know more. She offered a cigarette, then candy, but the dealer shook his head at both. "So how long did they have you locked up?"

"Nearly sixteen months."

"*Amazing!* And did your wife come and see you?"

"Well, no—you see, Patricia, she wanted done with me, and so she was getting a divorce."

"Did you have any children?"

"Yes, sadly. We had three."

"And she took 'em."

"Yes, yes."

"And now you're alone."

"Well, no, actually I've remarried, Patricia."

"Really!" Pat laughed in pure rejoicing at such a flow of news. The dealer looked up sharply, his eyes already narrowed with apprehension. But Pat took no notice. "How long ago was that?"

"What? Which? I came out of hospital four years ago and was married six months after."

"And you have more children?"

The dealer rallied at this friendly question. "Yes, Patricia, three more. I call it the second dynasty. The first family, you see, was the first dynasty, and this family now is the second."

"So you've had six children!"

"Yes, yes . . ."

"My God! Has any of your wives ever had an abortion?"

The dealer sat stunned for a minute, then turned slowly to me. "Will you please tell Patricia that she is carrying this a bit far?" he said in a barely audible voice.

"Oh, don't worry about me," Pat laughed. "I ask everybody that same question."

"That's true," I said. "If you had told her you weren't married, she would have asked you if you were a virgin."

"I would have, too," Pat said on another wave of laughter. "You should have seen Pamela Beardsley when I asked her. She's an old maid and a very good-looking woman, but I don't think she's ever had one affair. Or maybe just one. She turned so *red* and she couldn't speak when I asked her."

"How very kind of you to inquire," the dealer whispered righteously.

"You mean it *wasn't* kind," Pat said quickly. "I know people think that, but I don't see why. It's fun to ask. You always wonder about those things, so why not ask?"

"Yes, I suppose that's true," the dealer said. "Except that it makes people uncomfortable, and that's not right, is it, Patricia?"

"No, no, it's not right. You're right. I shouldn't have done it. I'm an evil woman to have done it and I hate to tell you that I'm sincerely sorry that I asked. But you still haven't told me. *Has* any of your wives had an abortion?"

8

PAT HUNTED up a copy of the *Daily Mirror* to confirm that it was really February—1967, just two years since the stroke: she couldn't bring herself to believe that Roald seriously intended to have her go out in public and give a speech with less than a month to prepare. It was going to be a gala dinner at the Waldorf in New York, an "Evening with Patricia Neal," in fact, where she would be the guest of honor, the featured speaker, the reason why everyone would be there. It was an impossible thing, and Pat had refused to get down to work on it, all through the fall.

Valerie Eaton-Griffith, a new friend in the village and the best and most determined of Pat's teachers, had done everything she could to coax Pat into thinking about the speech and what it meant to her. The evening was dedicated to bettering the lot of brain-injured children, a cause Pat cared about so directly . . . But Pat resisted Val as well as Roald, balking even at rehearsing after Roald and Val wrote the whole speech for her.

Pat was incredulous when she learned that the idle agreement she'd given Roald was being taken as a firm commitment—the programs were already printed, Roald said. How could she possibly get out of it? She had also agreed to return to America for the Oscar ceremonies in Los Angeles a few weeks later; already the television network had written to ask what color gown she would wear. That was fun! That was exciting! The Oscar show would require just a couple of words from her, and she could look forward to it without a trace of worry. The dinner, though, was something she dreaded and preferred not to think about.

"You'd better get with it," Roald warned her. "If you make a botch of it, it'll be curtains for you. All those film moguls in the audience will just say, 'Well, that's it, she's through.' "

"And they'll be right," Pat answered. "I *cannot* remember lines! I *cannot* give a speech!"

"But you agreed to do it, Pat."

"I didn't! *You* agreed for me. I didn't say one word."

"That's hardly the point. The point is that they are counting on you. It will be a very great pity when you let them down."

The true, terrible physical humiliation of making a fool of herself in front of all her friends began to creep up on Pat as the days slipped by. She began to give a little time to reading through the speech, making Roald wince to hear how she stumbled over the same words time and again, losing her place, lapsing from comprehension, getting angry all around. She was so resigned to failure that her mood defeated every rehearsal until the big evening was only days and hours away.

Then Pat mustered a kind of energy within herself that had gone unused since the stroke. Instead of playing bridge with Val or poring over the atlas and encyclopedia (with Val doing most of the poring and Pat sitting by, kept awake by her sense of propriety as much as true curiosity), Pat began to work like a professional. The speech never left her hands, and she read it to Roald at supper after working on it with Val all day. Val was going to accompany her to New York, leaving Roald to stay with the children, and Val, too, had prepared a short speech to introduce Pat.

A week before departure day, Pat and Val held the closest imitation of a dress rehearsal they could manage within the confines of greater Great Missenden. They invited a dozen-odd friends and neighbors to St. Martin's, the stately house where Val lived with her sister and father, and before settling down to an evening of bridge and brandy, the guests assembled in a bank of chairs and listened with delight while the two speeches were read. Val was tremendously nervous, which made her voice sound remarkably like the Queen's. But Pat, astonishingly, was smooth and practiced, and she gave an almost flawless reading.

Pat was amazed by the show of interest that greeted her in New York. Flowers in her suite. Telephone messages from everyone. She had three days in town before the night of the banquet, and nearly all her time was taken up with interviews. Her spirits were high, and she did her best to be both honest and funny with the reporters. But the interviews came out sounding very bleak. When the man from the *Times* asked her if she was eager to return to motion pictures, she told him—"No, my husband's making me do it. I have no enthusiasm. I don't care. My husband's making a living and I'm spending it."

As it turned out, the banquet was a cinch. Standing in the wings waiting to go on, Pat felt perfectly calm and ready. Even when she strode across the stage, conscious of her limp and praying it wasn't too conspicuous beneath her floor-length gown, even in that first moment of showing herself to the gilded roomful of friends and important strangers, Pat felt not the slightest trace of fear. It was not precisely that she felt confident. Instead, she was empty of fear, and its absence left her able to stride right up to the podium and face the music, whatever it was to be. The thundering applause was like a warming quilt wrapping itself around her softly and with love, and before she could break through it to speak her first word she knew that nothing could go wrong. She saw that everyone in the room was on his feet for her—a standing ovation; the phrase was intact in her mind.

The Oscar show was less trying still, and there she was again rewarded with a standing ovation, which cost the network, it was said, forty thousand dollars in air time revenue. In Hollywood, as in New York, she divided her time between old friends and reporters, so that when she left for home, the entire country had had a glimpse of her, and most of those who saw her concluded that her recovery was all but complete.

✿

Mr. Wigley, the village constable, and as tall and handsome a policeman as one might ever be likely to meet, did not inspire Theo. Neither did Wally, the master builder of Gipsy House, who only that week had scaled tall ladders to mend the ravages of winter on the roof. Nor did Mr. Thurgar, the knowledgeable druggist, nor Michael Cook's father, a driver of heavy trucks, unduly impress this discriminating boy. He showed no interest in the work of his uncles—John, the stockbroker; Alex, the vet; or Leslie, an amateur architect and armchair scholar. Not even Roald, fighter pilot-author-gardener-gamesman that he was, could strike a spark of emulation in his son. But Theo had an idol, and he was Tibbs, the impeccable butler at Moyne Park, an imposing Essex estate belonging to Roald's old friend, Ivar Bryce.

Theo was a great advocate of black shoes, somber suits, sober ties, and Tibbs was the only man he knew who invariably came up to his sartorial standards. When Roald was dressed for an evening out, a crestfallen look often came into Theo's eyes, and sometimes he went to the extreme of throwing himself at his father's feet to tug off the offending oxblood field shoes with the spongy rubber soles. But whenever the family went over to spend a weekend at Ivar Bryce's mansion near the village of Bird Brook—where they were now spending Easter, after Pat's return from New York—Theo always found Tibbs precisely as he had left him—elegant, even beautiful, in black shoes, black suit, black tie.

Several guests had been invited as well, and after dinner, with Theo straining to help, Tibbs was fussing with a tape recorder while Pat herded the company into Ivar's magnificent library. "You've really got to hear this," she said as they filed in. "It's beautiful. It really is."

"I've heard the bloody thing about fifty times," Roald said diffidently, his back turned to the room. He was examining his favorite object in Ivar's opulent house, a plain crystal paperweight engraved with the millionaire owner's marvelous motto: IT IS BETTER TO INCUR A MILD REBUKE THAN TO ASSUME AN ONEROUS TASK."

Pat went on undeterred, beaming and ebullient as she explained to the guests what they were about to hear. The tape was wonderful, and her love of hearing it played could not be restrained by worrying about who else wanted to hear it. It was as if the speech and its reception had not quite registered on her in New York and it was only through the tape that she discovered how spectacularly good she really had been.

"I gave the *main speech,*" Pat said. "It was a huge dinner for—oh, so many people. It was a dinner that the . . . brain people had."

"The Brain-Injured Children," Roald corrected. "It's a big charity in the United States. The dinner was Pat's return, you see—'An Evening with Patricia Neal' they called it. No one had seen her in public since her illness, so it was a comeback after two years away."

"And this was their first big affair and they made so much money," Pat said. "So *many* people came to it. All my old friends. Anne Bancroft and Marion Goodman and Anne Jackson and the Cusicks—"

"Pat, they don't know these people," Roald said from his corner.

"No—well, never mind. They were all there, anyhow, and the mayor of New York gave me a medal. For my *courage,* mind you." She laughed gaily to dispel any hint of bragging, but the half-dozen house guests nodded and hummed sincere congratulations all the same. They were country gentry, unused to Pat's style of exaggeration, overstatement and kidding.

"So let's hear it," Roald said. Tibbs started the machine, then left the room, shadowed by Theo. There was a minute of crackling static that suddenly became a roar of applause, rolling on and on, a hero's welcome, a noise like the sound of surf. "They were giving me a standing ovation," Pat happily explained. Then the applause receded and Pat's recorded voice filled the room: *"I thank you, I thank you, I thank you."* Another breaker of applause came crashing in through the speakers.

"Look at her!" said Roald. "She's eating it up for the fiftieth time."

"Shhh—listen!" said Pat. But he was right, she knew it: she was glorying then and glorying now, unembarrassed to live and relive to the hilt the emotion of that moment, standing on the podium, her fear and nervousness vanished, legs strong, eyes clear, cheeks aflame with the crowd's adoration; she could hear this tape with pleasure a hundred times a day. Roald laughed affectionately, and the others all smiled. Wait till they hear what's coming, she thought. It gets better as it goes along.

"I hope what happened to me never happens to any of you." The words were spoken slowly, skillfully phrased for the best effect, the deep umber voice taking full command. *"It was* evil." Cheers, applause, even whistles here, mystifying the attentive circle in the library. Pat would have liked to stop the machine and explain the reference that made "evil" such a combustible joke. Valerie had introduced her

with a modest speech that recounted their work together over the past year: "I was very apprehensive when I first met Pat . . . I had two things to overcome, my tremendous shyness with strangers and the amateur's extreme uneasiness in such situations . . . but Pat and I were jolly lucky because a friendship sprang up between us. The sheer inertia of her condition was shocking. There were certain words she fell in love with and used over and over . . . 'evil' was one of these words . . . we came down on it like a ton of bricks and Pat has since stopped using it . . ." And thus Val, with her short, simple talk and dignified delivery had set Pat up for the evening's first laugh, a fine gag, nicely executed. She remembered how they had laughed.

"This thing burst in my head and from that moment on two people took over my life. First there was Roald, who knew what had happened and immediately telephoned exactly the right person, a neurosurgeon. He was the second person. He saved my life—he did—he and that splendid UCLA hospital in California. It wasn't only a fine operation. It was also a brave one. I know very well that the doctor thought I would conk out in the middle of it. [Nervous laughter in both banquet hall and library] *But Tennessee hillbillies don't conk that easy.* [Laughter and cheers] *And so I stayed alive . . .*

"Roald told them what to teach me. Reading, writing, arithmetic—the works. It was just like school all over again, only tougher, much, much tougher. God, they were marvelous people. Month after month they came . . . helping me to do things properly again. They came to help me, these people in our village, just because they wanted to. They came because they knew I was in trouble and because they

were our friends and neighbors. They honestly didn't care about my having been in films—nobody in our village took much notice of that, anyway. They came because I needed help. They came for free. For love. And I'll remember them till the day I die . . ."

The library was perfectly still save for the measured, ringing voice from the machine. Here were the answers to questions one didn't dare ask. It was impossible to meet this celebrated actress without wondering about all the horrors she had been through. She was certainly approachable—effusive, actually, and terribly frank and direct. But perhaps that was some residue of her illness. Perhaps her charming laughter and gaiety would crack if one probed for the details. One didn't know. One didn't dare ask.

"So this is where I have a small suggestion to make. To all husbands whose wives have had a stroke; to all wives whose husbands have had a stroke; to everyone in the same boat: Don't try to do it all yourself. *Roald didn't. He reserved his strength for running the house and family, and for earning a living. He couldn't have managed alone, so he got others to do the actual teaching. So my message to all of you is simply this: try calling up your friends. Ask them to come by for an hour a day, or just once a week. On schedule, mind you! Enough of them to keep the patient busy from nine to six every day. That's eight friends, or ten or twenty friends—a lot of friends, you may be thinking. But you would be very pleasantly surprised to discover how willingly people will join in and come to help you . . ."*

It was true enough, Pat thought; and yet the idea had sounded less convincing in New York than it did here in

England. She often wondered what her recovery would have been like had New York been the magnet that finally attracted them. They had friends in New York who would gladly cross the ocean for them, but could Roald have organized a full roster of teachers out of those busy lives? She doubted it, but maybe so; Roald had a fantastic knack for summoning help in a crisis. She smiled to herself, thinking of how expertly he would cajole his sisters on the telephone: "Were you thinking of coming over today? . . . Really? . . . Splendid! Well, ah—sort of when-ish?" Yes, the impulse to sound the gong was something he had taught her. Left to herself, she was more likely to turn inward on her hurt, as if a feeling of guilt made any kind of illness or grief a thing to be ashamed of.

"I worked with my friends in the village for six months. Then two things happened. First, I had a baby. A perfect baby. Her name is Lucy. Second, I got fed up with working so hard. I felt certain that I was as good as I'd ever be. I was about eighty percent recovered. Still plenty of problems. But I was really ready to take a breather. I wanted to give up and lie back and do nothing. And that's exactly what I would have done if Roald hadn't made me go on. I had reached the danger point. The point where so many people stop work and just cruise along. ["Cruise" was Roald's word; some cruise, Pat thought.] *That's what I wanted to do—cruise along. But the slave driver I live with said no, no, no . . ."*

An interesting twist of the truth, Roald thought. The speech was false when he wrote it, but it became true in the act of being spoken. Saying that Pat was eighty percent recovered six months after the aneurysm was merely a bit of morale building. Listening to her now, though, he could believe, with something more solid than faith alone, that the full recovery was finally in her grasp; she had done it, it was hers—if only she could be made to believe it.

"Instead, Roald just changed the routine. He canceled school. No more people came to the house to teach me. And that's where Val came in. I started going to her house two or three afternoons a week. And I've been going ever since. And I love it. I look forward to it. Slowly and cunningly, she nudged me forward. The work gets harder and harder. But Val is such a super sort of person that it's a joy to work with her . . .

". . . and now I want to say something about brain-injured children. I can only speak for our son, Theo. Theo has had eight operations since his accident. He developed hydrocephalus, and for the first four and a half years of his life he had a whole series of little valves put into his head. When they took the last one out, we sat by his bed in the hospital for ten days, watching for all the bad signs. They didn't return. And since then Theo has been doing beautifully. [Theo, leaning against the doorjamb, cast his eyes down bashfully.] *Naturally, we don't know for sure about his future. But we think he's doing jolly well. He's going to a normal school with children his own age. And he loves it. The only thing he can't master is drawing, but he's making progress. He is learning to be left-handed, and this is a tremendously difficult task. But Theo seems unburdened by it or by anything else. He's the most cheerful one of us all. In fact, he's the most cheerful person I know.* [This was too much; Theo fled.] *Theo's courage has been a real inspiration to me, and I've needed it . . .*

"And so you can see why I feel so close to the aims of this

society. And I want to thank all of you for coming here tonight—some of you from very far away." These last words were spoken with a special inflection, as though to suggest that "far away" could mean a state of mind as much as an address. The answering applause burst into the library with startling impact—another standing ovation. There was something in the quality of the sound it produced which made it clear that many in the audience were crying with joy and relief.

"Really very beautifully done, Pat," said Ivar, and every head nodded agreement. Tibbs materialized from the hallway and shut off the machine.

"Really, Pat, fantastically moving," said one of the ladies.

"I thank you, I thank you, I thank you," said Pat, imitating the opening of the speech. If the tape had run on a bit further, past another couple of minutes of applause, they could have heard the rest of it—Mayor Lindsay breaking through to present Pat with her medal: "Her Inspiring Courage and Renowned Achievements Merit Our Highest Esteem." Pat had responded simply. "Thank you," she said. "It's a nice, nice medal." Then came cheers and more applause and the sound of scraping chairs, which meant that it was over. She had never dreamed it would go so well, that she could face that roomful of all the people dearest and most important to her without the slightest trace of stage fright and deliver her speech as though she had written it herself. She had, in fact, made a few small changes. The three thank-yous were hers, and so, of course, was the line saying "Roald is a great man, I love him." The audience had liked that, had liked the whole speech so much. She couldn't get over the applause. The morning after the banquet she had asked Valerie about it: "Valerie, did they stand up when you came out too?" And when Valerie said no, she couldn't help being pleased all over again.

"It's bridge, then, is it?" said Ivar. They filed out to the cardroom and were soon absorbed in the game. When Pat passed her partner's forcing bid, Roald looked intense.

"You must answer your partner with a bid if you've got some points in your hand, Pat," he said sharply. "You do know how to count points, do you not?"

Do you not! It was hard to tell when he talked like that whether or not he was kidding. Who besides Roald could keep a straight face saying things like "You do, do you not?" It was partly for the benefit of Ivar, who as Pat's partner was the only injured party—if indeed there was an injured party; Pat studied her hand but could not see where her bidding had been wrong. It was probably just Roald showing off. He liked to make people think that he was tough with her. He was a far less difficult man when they were alone. Sometimes it seemed that he got into quarrels in public simply to escape the boredom of making small talk. And he loved to shock people, as at dinner that night when he had told Lady Milford-Haven about how they put saltpeter in the prisoners' porridge "lest buggery become endemic." That was Roald's idea of table talk, and it always made people laugh. He was really jolly good at it, he was amazing, a gr-r-reat man . . .

"For God's sake, Pat, do something." It was Roald again, being beastly.

"*Okay, okay*. What was it I bid?"

"You passed."

"I thank you so much for remembering. And I'm not meant to do that—"

"Not on a forcing bid unless your hand is an absolute shambles."

"So-o-o-o . . ." No two face cards in any one suit, and no suit longer than the two-three-four-five diamonds. Five diamonds topped by the jack. Should she answer in diamonds? But no—Jesus! The jack was a heart, not a diamond. She transferred her cards to her right hand, freeing the left for the delicate task of slipping out the jack and putting it where it belonged. That gave her . . . the queen and jack of hearts, four hearts in all. Four hearts, four diamonds, the ace of spades and four clubs—all in all, that was . . . eleven high-card points. She heaved a worried sigh. "I'll say . . . three hearts."

"Thank God," said Roald.

Roald's partner was the next one to bid. "Pass," she said instantly, as though the word were a soft explosion just behind her teeth.

Ivar bid four hearts, "Double," said Roald.

Roald doubled more often than anyone she knew. He did it hoping that the added risk would jinx you. It was a good trick, but not as good as he thought it was. You weren't supposed to double every time. "They're cooked," Roald told his partner as he led a queen. Pat was dummy, and she laid her cards out on the table in four rough columns which Roald straightened and pushed closer to Ivar's reach.

"You made a good bid, Patricia," Ivar said, picking up a card.

"Yes, just right," said the girl, what's-her-name, Roald's

partner—what *was* her name? There was nothing more annoying than always being at a loss for names. I've hated her for years, Pat thought, and now that I finally like her I can't remember her name. Her husband had to do with horses or betting, and she had something funny about her eyes, a look that was classy and cold. Years before, people like whoever-she-was had scared Pat silly. They had made her feel so *American,* really like a dumb girl from the South. These . . . good English families. A *good family:* she never used to care about family, and she really didn't now. Except that it was jolly lucky if you came from one. But well-born people didn't frighten her any more. Roald had got her out of that. Roald was a super snob who looked down on all the snobs.

Ivar made his bid and then some, and that set the pattern for the evening. They played for two hours, with Tibbs and his colleague William bringing coffee and drinks, and the game running on at a soft, easy pace that Pat found well within her command. Roald heckled her, of course, but in the end it was he who lost—the best player in Buckinghamshire, swearing like a sailor at his miserable cards. That made Pat very happy, and when she went to bed that night she slept for thirteen hours.

"Now, when you find the eggs, run quickly back and put them in the baskets. All the chocolate eggs. There are about forty of them, plus one egg that is jade. The child who finds the jade egg may keep it for himself, but please bring all the chocolate eggs together so that we may draw lots and share them equally." Roald listened with amusement as Ivar set forth the rules of his annual Easter egg hunt to the thirteen squirming children, who were dying to get on with it but too polite to let it show. They were a rare breed of youngsters, pink-cheeked and fair and outrageously well behaved. The Milford-Havens' two children were there—the Earl of Medina, age seven or so, and Lady Anne, about four—and there may well have been another peer or two among the others. It was odd how one felt a bit sorry for them, imprisoned as they were by their manners and their Bond Street playclothes. Compared to the rest of this fashionable assembly, Tessa and Theo and Theo's friend Michael looked positively scruffy.

Then they were off in all directions, racing past the sculptured hedges of the formal garden, down to the arbor, along the grassy bank of the stream. Ivar, dressed in pastel tweeds that were in perfect taste for supervising an Easter egg hunt, followed along at a slow morning stroll, carrying a large and pretty wicker basket. He probably had spent two weeks and a good hundred pounds organizing the hunt. The eggs were Cadbury's finest, some of them as big as footballs and filled with assorted candy. The jade egg was surely genuine, an egg the size of a cricket ball that might be worth fifty pounds itself.

It was incredible the way Ivar lived. His wife was almost always away, leaving him to rattle around in the sixty or seventy rooms of the manor house, the rambling garage full of Rollses and Jaguars, the marvelous whitewashed stable that was beginning to win some big races. For Ivar, the birth of a valuable foal bore all the excitement and importance that another man could feel only for a child.

The Earl of Medina found the jade egg, and soon children from all corners of the garden were bringing chocolate eggs for Uncle Ivar's basket. Within half an hour all but two had been found, and these were abandoned to the luck of the hunt. The children gathered in front of the twelve-foot fireplace in the main hall, where Ivar was waiting with all the hearts from a deck of cards in his hand—thirteen cards for thirteen children—with the number, from ace to deuce, giving each child his place in the order of choosing. The chocolate bounty was spread out on the carpet; three giant eggs with filigreed icing dwarfed all the rest.

Theo drew the queen, for third place, but Theo being Theo, bypassed the rich prize that remained and went instead for a small proletarian egg.

"You can have the big one, Theo," Ivar said, but Theo was caught in mid-stride on his way to show Michael his prize, and he shook his head no.

"You're sure?"

"Yes, I'm sure," said Theo. It was already too late for him to change his mind, anyway; the Earl of Medina, holder of the jack, was lugging his booty back to his armchair.

"Ah, you always come out on top, don't you?" said Lord Milford-Haven, ruffling his son's fine blond hair.

They started for home early in the day, wanting to spend part of Easter with Lucy and Ophelia, who had been left at home with Joyce and Tini, the new cook and nurse. Joyce was from the West Indies and Tini was Dutch, and together they made the best team Gipsy House had ever had. Klara and Rita had been closer to Pat's heart than any of the other girls, but then Rita left to learn secretarial work and "better herself," and Klara was summoned home to Hungary under threat of Kafkaesque reprisals if she stayed. Rita landed a job in Mersham and was boarding with Marjorie Clipstone, so she was still a frequent visitor to the house. And from Klara came wonderful letters that made Pat yearn for her salty good company: "I tell you something. Everyone knew, here in Hungary, that you have been in New York. At the newspaper where I work we have got the news and your photo the same day as you arrived. We put an article and the photo in the paper of course. You know, you are very popular here in Hungary since I got back from England and made a good propaganda for you. OK, I know you don't need propaganda. But here, in Hungary, you do . . ."

The new girls were as good, if not better, at their jobs, however. Tini was in her early thirties, a pretty blonde with a brisk, cheerful manner and a great capacity for work. Joyce had just arrived from Jamaica, where Pat and Roald had met her on a winter holiday, and she was still showing signs of bad culture shock. She was a Southern Baptist and a righteous one, unused to proximity with cigarettes and spirits, let alone the vile language and bawdy humor that sometimes escaped her employers' lips. As a black girl in Buckinghamshire, Joyce was marooned, save for small pockets of Jamaicans in High Wycombe and in Holmer Green, a village above Little Missenden. She was a professional home economist, as attested by the framed diploma that hung on the wall above her bed.

The children sang "Chitty Chitty Bang Bang" in hysterical falsetto as Roald steered the stately Rover along the softly curving road that led home across Cambridgeshire. They were on their five-hundredth chorus, and the search for funnier ways to sing it had long since gone dry. A few miles back he had told them solemnly that they were among a handful of select children the world over who knew the

"Chitty Chitty" song, having learned it from a tape recording ("a secret tape," he said) made by the composers for Roald's use in his work on the screenplay. *Chitty* was his second big movie, a seventeen-million-dollar adaptation of another slender Ian Fleming book, and Roald was getting not only more money and a percentage of the profits but also an even freer hand. There was so little to the story that you could almost take the name and the basic idea (a magic car) and enlarge upon it until the screenplay became very much your own. The volcano he had written into *You Only Live Twice* (and which, to his total amazement, had been constructed in more or less full scale on a back lot at Pinewood Studios—the most expensive single set ever built, it was claimed) now housed a vast candy factory, and a number of other extravagant fancies that had struck him were already under design. He was enjoying his part in building a children's fantasy into a movie and he felt completely engaged by the work. If he wrote just one more film after this one, he could put enough money in the children's trust fund to free his mind for his own real work. Financial security was the one thing he needed to settle down to writing enough new stories to complete a third collection on a par with *Kiss Kiss* and *Someone Like You*—three years' work at the very least. He would welcome it, he was ready for it, he needed to return to his craft. His old fear of going stale from cranking out too many stories had vanished from his mind, quite possibly because he had written only two really serious stories in the past six or seven years. No, he was hardly in danger of going stale. The more real threat was allowing himself to become seduced by his splendid new earning power. On the strength of his two finished screenplays, he was already among the top-money Hollywood writers.

"Will you *stop that noise!*" Pat wrenched around in the seat to face the silenced children. Tessa and Theo looked momentarily stricken and ashamed, but Michael could not stop grinning. Michael was four years older than Theo, but his sense of humor didn't show it. He was every bit as silly as his small friend, and every bit as cheerful in his mischief. Michael you had to clout to show that you were angry. "You, too, Michael, all three of you. That song is driving me dotty."

"Can we sing it quietly, Mummy?" Tessa asked in a voice meant to advertise how quietly she was planning to sing.

"Just *stop it now,*" said Pat, turning back to the unwinding road ahead.

"May we sing something else?"

"Tessa! You are making me very angry. You stop asking, do you understand?"

"Yes, Mummy," Tessa answered in an injured tone that was like a spoken pout.

"I sincerely hope so." Pat sounded weary as well as cross.

The children stayed quiet for a mile or two, but then giggles and whispers announced the invention of a nonsense game that soon filled the car with a racket more tortuous than any song:

"Hello, Mr. Potato."

"Hello, Mrs. Cabbage."

"This is Mr. Turnip, Mr. Potato."

"Oh, how *do* you do, Mr. Turnip?"

"Fine, thank you, Mr. Potato. How do *you* do? How does Mrs. Cabbage do?"

Pat was about to explode when Roald felt a tremor of her anger.

"Listen, you nippers," he said. "Who would like to climb up Ivinghoe Beacon?"

"Me!"

"Oh, yes, Daddy—super!"

"Right, then; we'll do it. Another ten minutes will get us there."

The trick worked: the children were already straining to see the first signs of arrival and the car fell quiet. Roald sucked contentedly on his pipe. They had climbed the high hill before. It was a steep hike up the Beacon's face, and from the top of it, several hundred feet above the road and the Ivinghoe village, you had the feeling that you could see all of England.

Pat glared at him a long while before speaking. "Ooooo, you make me so angry, Roald. Why do you always . . . let them win?"

"Let them win?"

"Yes, you do. They were being rotten children and you reward them for it." Tessa had her chin hooked on the soft leather backrest behind Pat's shoulder, but she didn't seem to hear what was being said. Theo and Michael, still staring out the window, had taken to outbidding each other for the honor of most times up the Beacon: "Ten times!" "Forty times!" "Five thousand times!" "A million times!"

"You can't just shout at them all the time," Roald argued. "First you have to learn to ignore them. You've got to put them out of your mind and let them amuse themselves. It's a long drive for a nipper, you know."

"Well, it's a long drive for me, too. I *happen* to have a headache."

"A headache you got because you had too much to drink last night."

Pat did not answer, which was most unusual for her. She was definitely on the side of ending fights with a bang, not a whimper. But now she was burning in silence. Perhaps this was the captive automobile passenger's equivalent of stalking off. Given such a wallop at home, she almost certainly would have flounced away, upstairs, back to her study, nursing her anger or hurt for an hour's hibernation, after which you could always induce her to forget it.

"We're here! We're here!" Theo shouted as Roald swung into the gravel parking lot at the base of the imposing hill, which stood out in the landscape around it like a pear on a plate. It was a fine, clear day, windy and brisk. A half-dozen gliders from the sailplane field at Dunstable floated overhead in gull-like silence.

"Have all you nippers got sweaters or coats?" Roald asked.

Yes, yes, yes. They scrambled out of the car, buttoning and bundling themselves up. Pat remained rooted in place.

"Aren't you coming with us?"

She turned her head majestically and looked through Roald, as though she couldn't be bothered to focus her eyes. "No," she said. *Noooo.*

"Oh, come on, you can do it. You would have been willing to do it when you still had the leg brace."

"You go. I want to stay here." It was definite. There was no use arguing. Roald led the children across the parking lot, then started up the grassy bank holding Theo's hand.

Michael bounded ahead. His friendship with Theo was

remarkable and rather touching, since he was not only older but far stronger and more agile, and leagues ahead in sports and games. Yet they played together every afternoon, and on weekend mornings it was usually Michael who brought in the papers. At first Roald had assumed that Michael simply tolerated Theo in exchange for having a fairly exciting refuge away from the crowded rooms in the council houses down the lane where his family lived; Michael had told everyone that he slept on the davenport in the living room and was never asleep before midnight, when his parents turned off the telly. But a year or more had passed without a flicker in the friendship, and it was obvious now that the two boys loved each other like brothers. Michael had even been overheard at the "Corner Caf'" naming Theo Dahl as his "best mate."

Occasionally Michael forgot himself and Theo got hurt in the action. But considering that he played on the school football team and was fierce as a cat among boys his own age, Michael displayed a real gift for tenderness in the way he looked out for Theo. He seemed to have unfailing intuition for Theo's limits and was often seen helping him along or holding him in check when the panting Theo taxed himself too far. The results, for Theo, were already spectacular. The last time they climbed the Beacon he had to be carried two thirds of the way. Now, with no more support than two steadying hands placed lightly around his rib cage, Theo scrambled all the way to the top.

The view from the top was enough to impress even the three children, who stood at the edge of the summit plateau and gasped at the distance they had climbed. The wind reddened their cheeks and pried at the buttons of their coats. They could even look down on some of the gliders that had circled into the valley. Theo spotted the forest-green Rover way below and waved mightily on the chance that his mother might be watching. Then they started down, hampered by their new awareness of height and danger, scuttling nervously from one handhold to the next. Michael finally went ahead on his own, leaping and skidding down the mountain-goat trail until he ran out safely at the bottom. But Tessa panicked and froze, touching off Theo's alarm, so that Roald could proceed only gingerly and after much calm persuasion, with Theo clutching a pants leg and Tessa tearing at the sleeve of his sweater. Fifty yards from the bottom, the children regained their nerve and ran on ahead of him. Theo fell in a classic spread-eagle belly flop but landed in tall grass and was quickly on his feet again, no damage done.

It was Tessa who started the chant going when they rolled into Great Missenden a half-hour later. Even on this sunny Easter afternoon, the place could have been a ghost town. Pat stared out the window at the shadowed storefronts as the others joined in with Tessa, one by one: "All the shops are *closed!* All the curtains *drawn!* All the doors are *locked!* All the people *gone!*" The children were bursting for the long ride to end, and they were out on the lawn playing Keep Away and shattering the quiet with their laughter before Pat could elbow the car door open and turn in her seat to swing her feet down onto the graveled drive.

Pat and Val had gone back to work right after their trip to New York, interrupted only by Pat's brief visit to Hollywood for the Oscar ceremony. They were fast friends now, and

Pat had invited Val to come with her again when she went back to New York to make *The Subject Was Roses,* which had originally been scheduled to start in the spring. It was now set for September, so they had a good six months to prepare. With a librarian's dedication, Val had been over the script a dozen times, cutting it up into morsels that Pat could master in a few days and setting up a timetable for the job of memorizing the scenes in which Pat would have a long speech or an extended bit of dialogue.

The trip they had taken together served them as a point of demarkation, and they did not go back to the reference books and atlases they had used before. "Lessons" were not so much what Pat needed now as exercise of the talents she had regained. When they did not work on the script, they wrote letters or played bridge or went over the newspapers together. And for Pat it was a very rewarding time. She had improved far more than she dared to believe until some concrete accomplishment made her progress undisputable.

With Val's help, Pat also composed a short recollection of her Kentucky birthplace requested by the Louisville *Courier-Journal:*

> I can remember a dirt road and a single-track railway. A little group of wooden shacks surrounding a general store. My father's office and behind it the pit head. I remember the creek in Packard where the water ran fast and cold over my feet as I waded knee-deep.
>
> And I remember the hills of rough grassland, rounded and pleasant. One of these hills sheered up steeply outside my bedroom window at the back of my doctor-grandfather's house. There was no running water in this house or any other. Just a potty in the garden. Bath time consisted of a whopping tin

tub drawn up by the kitchen range. And this in a mining town where the men came home to their wives with coal dust all over them.

The railroad ran slap between the fifty or so houses, virtually taking the place of a High Street. Roses and chrysanthemums grew in the little front gardens.

My grandfather was a general practitioner of the old kind. With no hospital in Packard, he had to be a regular one-man band, doing everything for his patients. He even preached to them in the church.

Everyone flocked to church on Sundays, very sure of their faith, and very posh in their best suits. They said "Amen, Amen," after everything, again and again, "Amen. Amen."

I loved the Bible as my grandfather read it to us, at home as well as in church. I used to ask a lot of questions, but my grandfather didn't like what he called "questioning the Bible," so I never got any answers.

I remember the Baptist church, the center of our lives, and how we all wore new white shoes every Easter Sunday. My family was always happy there.

I remember a kind of concrete strip in front of the store. Men gathered there to yarn; women, too. It was a sort of village pass-the-time-of-day place. The mine, the church and the store—these were the centers of activity in Packard.

I remember playing on the tracks and in the stream and climbing the hills. I remember a curious small girl vowing to remove a wart from my hand by a spell. I agreed. She said secret words, then buried an old rag and as it rotted the wart faded away.

I'm not sure what you will find if you return to Packard. When I last heard, the house where I was born was about the only thing left standing.

Was that sort of what they wanted? Pat read it over again. She was amazed at how much and how well she remembered; she could recall the tiniest things, anything that had ever happened to her—everything except the names. If she had worked harder at it she could have remembered even more, like the way the store smelled, the company store, full of meal and lard and huge bolts of cotton and bags of nails—she could have described the whole store, a place she hadn't seen in thirty years.

Everything in the letter was true. It was a fine letter but the words were . . . funny. *Potty*—did she say "potty"? That's right, she did. She could hear herself saying it. She started saying "potty" when she had babies. Before that she must have said . . . "john." "The john." And *gardens*—she used to say "yards." In England they called a yard a garden even if it was nothing but grass, like a yard. *Garden* and *High Street* and *posh* and *curious little girl* showed how English she was getting to be, although "posh" and "curious" sounded like words Valerie had put in. In America they said "strange" or "funny" or "crazy" for *curious*. And in England, for "crazy" they said "dotty." She said "dotty" herself, like in "You are driving me dotty."

But her own letters, the ones she made up and typed herself, sounded different, she thought. Not half as good, probably. She liked to write letters and sometimes said things in them that made her laugh to herself as she wrote. If you could call it writing, the way she sat at the typewriter, hunting for the letters and picking them out with her left finger, her left . . . index finger. It was more like doing a puzzle or crocheting than really sitting down to write.

There was so much mail she wanted to answer. She had to write immediately to her mother and her beloved Aunt Maude. Her mother's letters made her laugh, and Aunt

Maude's were amazing, with everything spelled exactly right and showing so much love for her. And there were tons of letters from people who just wanted to know her; she had to send them a post card at least. Some of them were fantastic. There was this woman in Ohio who wrote her a letter every week, never less than ten pages, and with two or three drawings of herself in colored pencil illustrating the things she described in the letter: "Here I am washing dishes after late TV." And Helen! She had to write a thank-you to poor Helen, whoever she was, Helen out on Long Island. Helen sent so many presents to the children and wrote long, long letters telling her everything about her life, as if they were close friends. So now she would have to write and say, "Thank you, thank you, you shouldn't have done it," when really it would be better and friendlier to say, "Poor sad Helen, get out of my life, we don't know each other, Helen, and you're wasting your money and time."

And she had to write to her agents. She was very cross with her agents, very disappointed. As soon as she became ill they had lost interest in her, but now that the producers of *Roses* wanted her, the agents were coming around again. Harvey Orkin had called just a day or two ago: "Hi, sweetheart, how's my lover?" She had told him what a rotten man he was, but now Roald said she had to write him a letter canceling her contract and send a copy to his boss. It wasn't enough to tell them on the phone. She had already typed the envelopes, with "Esq." after their names, but Roald would have to tell her what to put in the letter.

Because of the postponement, the *Roses* people had offered to pay her twenty-five thousand dollars extra just for promising not to make another movie before they got started.

Nobody had ever paid her *not* to work before. And there wasn't much chance of working, anyway. The only offer she had was to be the mother of . . . Oedipus? Yes, it was Oedipus, Oedipus' mother in an English film. But everyone agreed that it would not be the right thing for her. She had to start working harder on the script of *The Subject Was Roses*. She and Val had done the first twenty pages, but now she had forgotten what little she had learned. The lines were very good, very short lines . . . short, short, short. So that was good. But she still would never learn them. They'll have to coach me and use cue cards, she thought, and even then I'll probably forget most of the lines. She felt sorry for the poor director—what was his name? She ought to know the director's name, and the leading men's names, but she could not remember them.

The deal for *The Subject Was Roses* had been set so long ago that it was hard for Pat to bring it into the focus of immediate reality. Roald had done all the talking when the producers came to Gipsy House around Christmas, and when the script arrived she hardly gave it any notice. Now months had passed by with the script lying around the house before she took an interest in looking at it. And now that she and Val were going at it every day, the shooting date was postponed again, this time from September until January. January 1968—once again the date seemed unreal to Pat, and she lost what momentum she had built up for the hard task of preparation.

Roald kept telling her that she *needed* to make another film, for her own sake. Otherwise she would never know where the outer limits of her capacities lay and would condemn herself to a smaller life than the one she had left behind. And that was true: she agreed, she agreed. But it was also true that she didn't really want to do it, although for a short while just after she came home from America, she had felt she could do anything and was eager to go to work again. But that time had passed, and now she wished more than anything that the whole thing would be dropped and forgotten. Sometimes it seemed to her that she would miss "being a star," but not all that much. She was happy enough with things as they were; she didn't need to prove anything to herself any more.

Still, if she did not work on the script, Pat found herself strapped for things to do. She had not regained the habit of reading, so Roald chose to make this her new soft spot and harangued her about it every chance he got. I had been away from Gipsy House for several months when I returned to spend a few days with Pat fresh from her triumphant visits to New York and Hollywood. She looked far better than the last time I saw her, but Pat was far from fresh. She was in a bad mood, a sad-joke mood, but also in a mood to talk:

"How's my reading? You don't want me to read to you, do you? I've been reading *The Diary of Anne Frank,* and my God, she was a good writer. It's so *sad,* all the things that happened to her. I get the sense of it, but I have to read so slowly. I think it's my eyes, not my mind. Every word I see I have known. When I read, I sometimes get—oh, what are they called? The sort of little words, sort of *and* and *but* and *was* and *is,* you know, I get them mixed up. I get lost in sentences.

"But it's time I got well again. I don't think my walk will ever be normal, which is sad, and Roald says it won't because

I don't do my exercises. And I don't because I get sick and tired of them. I walked to the village yesterday with Lucy, and we shopped, and do you know, it took us two hours. And we didn't even stop for coffee. I go so *slowly*.

"I have trouble with my foot and ankle and even the leg—it doesn't work right. Nothing hurts, though. I can walk for a long time without it hurting. The rotten thing is keeping my shoe on. Every time I walk, *boing, boing, boing*—it flaps down and my heel is out on top of the shoe all the time.

"Roald is a rotten man and so are you. You haven't even heard the tape of my speech, which was *jolly good,* I'll tell you.

"I'm sorry to be leaving my four children with their father this summer. I sincerely hope they'll miss me, but they probably won't.

"*Roald* has taken over everything, and I can't get back in. I'm so angry with him. I've been nothing for so long, but now I'm something, and I want you and Roald to know it."

9

GREAT MISSENDEN
DECEMBER 1, 1967

MY BELOVED FRIENDS,

I AM WRITING TO ALL OF YOU AT THE SAME TIME. PLEASE FORGIVE ME, BUT SO MUCH HAS HAPPENED THAT I HAVE TO DO IT THIS WAY.

FIRST OF ALL, ROALD HAD A SPINAL OPERATION ON NOVEMBER 4TH. HE WAS IN GREAT PAIN WHEN I TOOK HIM TO THE HOSPITAL IN AN AMBULANCE. THEY OPERATED ON HIM THE NEXT MORNING. THE WOUND DID NOT CLOSE AND HE BLED MANY TIMES, WHICH RESULTED IN HIM HAVING A SECOND OPERATION ON NOVEMBER 21ST. THIS OPERATION WAS SUCCESSFUL AND WITH THE HELP OF BLOODTRANSFUSIONS, 6 PINTS, HE IS NOW ON THE MEND I DO BELIEVE.

HE IS IN AN OXFORD HOSPITAL WHERE NESTA POWELL NURSES. SHE HAS BEEN A TREMENDOUS HELP TO HIM. SHE IS A GREAT WOMAN.

ROALDS BELOVED MAMA DIED ON NOVEMBER 17, THE FIFTH

ANNIVERSARY OF OUR OLIVIAS DEATH AND WAS BURIED THE SAME DAY AS OLIVIA.

HOW SAD, HOW VERY, VERY SAD.

TESSA IS BOARDING NOW AT ROEDEAN SCHOOL. ONLY LAST WEEK SHE GAVE IN THAT SHE LIKES IT ENORMOUSLY, WHICH MAKES US ALL VERY HAPPY. WE ARE NOW SURE THAT SHE WILL FINISH HER SCHOOLING AT ROEDEAN.

THEO IS A GREAT BOY. HE IS DOING EXCEEDINGLY WELL AT SCHOOL. WE DO NOT KNOW YET WHERE HE WILL FINISH WITH HIS EDUCATION, BUT WE HOPE IT WILL BE A DAY SCHOOL AND NOT A BOARDING SCHOOL.

OPHELIA IS GOING TO GATEWAY A VILLAGE SCHOOL AND SHE LOVES IT.

LUCY IS SO RIGHT AND BEAUTIFUL I CAN NOT TELL YOU. SHE SEEMS TO BE ALMOST LIKE OLIVIA. SHE MAKES UP POEMS JUST LIKE HER.

THEY ARE BOTH DEVINE GIRLS.

ALTHOUGH I AM RECOVERING FROM A BAD FLU, I AM JUST FINE.

AND SO I SEND YOU ALL MY LOVE AND WISH YOU ALL A VERY HAPPY CHRISTMAS, KNOWING WE ARE SO NEAR TO IT.

PAT

"Oh, dear," said Roald from his hospital bed. "You haven't sent out a great many of these, have you?" His neck was held in traction by a canvas harness attached to a length of clothesline that ran through a pulley above his head to an eleven-pound weight that dangled just behind the bedstead. The harness gripped him around the forehead and under the chin, forcing him to stare endlessly up at the cracks in the ceiling and to lift the lead weights with his jaw muscles every time he spoke.

"I don't know—about twenty," said Pat. "I typed it twice with two carbons and Edna did the rest." Edna was Pat's secretary, a new addition to the staff—Edna Groves, whose husband, Mike, was gatekeeper at the Great Missenden railway station and sometimes worked in the garden at Gipsy House in place of the departed Lambert.

"I do hate these Christmas letters," Roald said, reaching back to make a few inches' slack in the rope so that his jaw would be free for talking. " 'This year our happy ménage was joined by three goldfish and a parakeet.' I hate the bloody things."

"Well, how was I supposed to let everyone know? I can't write a letter to each one." Pat was indignant. She was proud of the work she had done to get the letter out, proud of the letter itself, especially in Edna's clear-typed copy.

"An individual post card with just a few lines is better than some mass-circulation broadside, the same bloody letter to all your friends," Roald said crossly. He released the rope, clamping his jaw firmly shut on the last word.

"Well, Roald, I'm very sorry to tell you that I disagree," Pat said, glaring down on him. "I couldn't agree less. Everybody wants to know everything that happened to us, and I haven't got time to write letters to everybody. Besides, you tell everybody the same thing any way you do it. They all want to know about you and how you're feeling and the children . . ."

But Roald had drifted off into communion with his pain. In his disciplined silence, Roald conveyed his suffering with terrible impact, so that the merest wince was equal to a scream. And he was wincing mightily. This kind of pain was something he hadn't bargained on. He had come in for the operation after several weeks of acute back pains, when his resistance was ready to give out. He was confident that the operation, for all its risk and cost to his strength, would at least bring an end to the stabbing ache in his back. But now the pain was worse than ever and when a wave of it was upon him he had to give in to it, riding it out, holding on with eyes shut and fists clenched while beads of sweat formed across the bridge of his nose. He had lost much weight and his face was like a death mask. The harness made red tracings along his cheeks, squeezing the skin into small gray pouches under each eye.

"Poor baby," Pat murmured. "Poor baby."

There was nothing whatever she could do. She hardly dared touch him or stroke his brow for fear of upsetting some delicate balance of wounded vertebrae. And to talk while he suffered so cruelly seemed the worse kind of intrusion on the privacy of his ordeal. There was nothing to do but stay with him until he fell asleep or spoke to her again or asked her to go. She had brought the mail from home, but the very sight of it had been enough to make him angry with her. He didn't want the apples or candy, either. She wished there were something she could do.

It was a shame he didn't like her having sent the letter. She had mailed it quite unaware of how severely it would test everyone's nerves. She had already reported Roald's debacle in telegrams to her family and half a dozen friends ("ROALD DOING WELL AFTER SPINE OP LOVE PAT" was the way they were received). She had sent them impulsively, knowing that Roald would have done the same. But even within the circle where it brought no surprise, the letter sent everyone reeling at the plain, impossible fact of more woe for the Dahls. No one could believe it. A rush of mail arrived and there were several frantic calls from America: Was it really true? Could it be as bad as it sounded? Pat told everyone that it was serious, all right, but she sounded prepared for whatever was in store for her, dramatically better and far more in charge of herself than she had been a few months before.

Roald's troubles with his back had begun at the end of what had seemed like an endless summer. The postponement of Pat's movie had given the family a stretch of free summertime no one had counted on, and since the weather was fine on the Continent and there was money in the bank, Roald declared a holiday. They would go to Guéthary, on the Bay of Biscay, for a month in the sun.

Theo broke his arm the week before they left, but that was nothing very alarming, least of all to Theo, who carried his cast like a shield. Once in France, they settled down to a restful cure at a fine hotel that was not a hundred yards from the beach. The great cuisine, the sun and the exercise and the uncounted hours put Roald in the best of form. He was full of energy and good humor, feasting every night, sampling all the wines, beating Angela Kirwin at tennis (a Bucks County finalist who was again part of the family's entourage), and Swifty Lazar at golf (who had breezed into Biarritz to sample the golf). Roald was also determined to ring down the curtain on the Biarritz casino with his Scarne blackjack system, and for days before his first night's venture, he spent great amounts of time dealing through all possible combinations of hands in order to rehearse his calls. "Hit me" or "No hit" he would say to himself, drawing long glances from hotel guests at tables near his on the porch. He took Pat with him for his first assault on the casino, only to be turned away at the door because Pat had not brought her passport for identification; moreover, blackjack was not among the games the casino offered. Roald turned away and trudged down the block-long carpeted marble corridor, livid with frustrated gambler's blood. But, emerging from the men's room at the far end of the hall a few minutes later, Roald had his full revenge. "THERE'S NO PAPER IN THE LAVATORY!" he shouted at the top of his voice, down by the casino doors. The attendants came running in panic, and Roald went home a happy man.

But idleness was poison to Pat, and as Roald's mood prospered, hers seemed to wane. She enjoyed the food and drank so many toasts to the chef that he was encouraged to stretch out to the limits of his art for ever more splendid dishes, doubling the bill as he went along. She played bridge in the evenings, charming and beguiling the serious French players with her Actors Studio approach to the game. And she stayed awake for the day-trips Roald plotted through the Spanish towns across the border and up into the foothills of the Pyrenees. But she would not swim or even sunbathe and she could not bring herself to look at her script or begin a book or think up amusements for the children. She slid back into the mental state that had plagued her off and on from the beginning, the minor key counterpoint to the obvious physical fact of her recovery, the depression, the morbidity, the sense of being done for. She slept too late and drank too much and fell into Faustian rambles on the death of her faith.

"We live alone. Alone! Alone!" she proclaimed one evening after supper. "I know that. I've known it since my illness."

"What do you mean, 'alone'?" Roald said. "You've only got to look around to see your family and your friends all around you."

"Yeah. But you're still alone. You're born alone and you die alone, and after you die, you're still alone."

"Ballocks," said agnostic Roald, rising to defend the faith. "You mean to tell me that you've thought it all through and decided that there is no God?"

"That's right, except I haven't had to think about it. I *know* it. You'd know it too if what happened to me had happened to you."

"It might be just a shade better, you know, if you told yourself there might be an afterlife. How do you know there isn't? We're surrounded by the inexplicable. You've only got to look at the sky at night and you see it. You see it! You don't have a hope of understanding it, and yet it's there."

"Or else it isn't there."

"But you can see it!"

"Yes, you can, but it doesn't mean anything. You can't make yourself believe in God if you don't. You can't pray to nothing."

"But why insist on God? You can pray to any spirit you want to believe in. Or if not precisely *pray,* then at least commune, or try to commune."

Pat burst into laughter. "*Commune!* I didn't know that you communed, Roald. Tell me, who is it you *commune* with?"

"None of your business."

"Come on," she said, rising up in her chair for more imposing leverage. "You better tell me."

"It's none of your business, Pat."

She sprang from her chair and was on him with tickling fingers digging for the ribs. "Come on, baby, you better . . ." she laughed as they struggled against each other.

"All right! All right!" Roald said, pushing her hands away. "I'll tell you. Olivia." The hush induced by the name fell across the table like a club. "That is, I try to. I tried to when we used to go to church."

Pat nodded. Roald smiled softly, holding Pat's gaze with his own. "Well, that's just what *I* do," he said. "You have to do what you can."

When the holiday was over, they returned to Great Missenden to get Tessa ready for her first year at Roedean, a big boarding school in Brighton, the alma mater of Roald's three sisters and Else's beautiful twins. Pat and Roald drove her down to Brighton, with the Rover packed full of new school clothes and the air thick with the pain of parting. The idea of Roedean was something they all had to adjust to, and their farewell was tearful and tender. It would be a month until they saw each other again, and that was as much as any of them could take. Letters came from Tessa every day plotting a graph that began with pleading and pining and gradually ascended, through various phases of resignation and acceptance, to reach at last the summit of schoolgirl success: fantastic friends, a nice headmistress, a place on the basketball team. Pat and Roald took turns writing back to her and the whole family missed her as much as their letters said.

Pat was killing the autumn much as she had killed the spring. The script stayed tucked in her cubbyhole by the kitchen table. Roald tried to interest her in tending to the orchids in the fine new greenhouse Wally had built next to the gypsy caravan, and for a few weeks it seemed as if he were making the first frail inroads on her well-established indifference to horticulture. But her heart wasn't in it, and when she let it slide she was left with only her familiar pastimes: the mail, bridge with Val and her sister Daphne, shopping in the village, taking naps. She was still a customer in a million along High Street, but now she was obsessed with the untidiness of the town. She would cross the street to pick up a discarded candy wrapper, and when she entered the shops she always carried a sordid bouquet of litter, to be deposited in the trash can. At home she was obsessed with fierce little economies and would complain hotly about lights left burning and the disappearance of milk or matches.

Roald had signed to write the *Brave New World* screenplay and was absorbed in the study of futuristic speculations on the year 2000 and beyond. But he could find no translatable plot in Huxley's novel and felt dissatisfied with the little work he had done. His neck was bothering him and he made several trips to London to be treated by chiropractors, or "manipulators," as he called them. He did not connect this new discomfort to the back troubles that had been haunting him for nearly twenty years. Right after the war he had had two operations, one of them a disastrously complicated misadventure, and the RAF pensioned him off as eighty percent disabled. In 1960, however, a physical therapist in New York had put him through a three-month course of exercise and treatment, and with his program of weight lifting and calisthenics to stabilize the cure, Roald had enjoyed the strongest and healthiest years of his life. It was not until the pain in his neck was replaced by a far deeper ache in the small of his back that Roald began to worry, and by then it was already hurting too much to permit him to think very clearly.

Roald's flair for quiet heroics made him an excruciating invalid to have around the house. He took to bed as reluctantly as a great oak falls, and within a few days was suffering so that he couldn't sit up without sweating. His right arm pulsed with needles of pain and went numb in the fingers and hand; his right leg slowly lost both feeling and strength. He would slither out of bed and drag himself across the carpet to the bathroom, clutching at the nap of the rug for a handhold and murmuring, "It's all right," and "Don't worry," as Pat stood by in horror. Wally was summoned to build a brace under the bed to make it firmer, but it was far too late for such a simple remedy. Roald writhed on in silence, watching soap operas on television or tuning in police calls on the Japanese AM-FM shortwave walkie-talkie. Theo, still under the spell of Tibbs, raced up and down the stairs with a tea towel over his arm, bringing food and drinks; as before, when Pat was bedridden, Theo seemed completely undisturbed by the presence of grave illness in the house.

In the midst of Roald's torment Pat was offered a part in another film, *The Stalking Moon,* starring Gregory Peck, a thoughtful Western in which she would play a frontier woman abducted and raped by Indian bandits, then rescued and morally rehabilitated by scout and born loner Peck. Since the role portrayed a woman in a state of deep shock following her maltreatment at the hands of the Indians, there was a minimum of dialogue. Pat loved the whole idea: Gregory Peck, a big production, a big salary and hardly any lines—her heart was set on it the minute the film was described. The only hitch was that it was scheduled to be shot during the same months that Pat had agreed to spend in New York making *The Subject Was Roses*.

Roald, too, thought that *The Stalking Moon* would make a splendid vehicle for her return, if only because her enthusiasm was so high for it. After all the postponements of *Roses,* she seemed unable to muster a spark of excitement for it, and that was beclouding her whole approach to returning to work. The trick would be to talk the *Roses* people into releasing her from her contract or postponing their production again until late spring, when Pat would have made *The Stalking Moon* and spent the Easter holidays with the children. From his sickbed Roald masterminded the subtle strategies involved, placing calls to Swifty and to the producers of the two pictures. Sometimes he did the talking on the phone, but more often he coached Pat from his side of the bed, holding up cue cards with telling points for Pat to recite to Hollywood or New York.

"I don't know what I'll do if I have to make that other film," Pat would say between calls. "This one is so beautiful. I know it's going to be a great, great picture."

"Well, you haven't really seen the script, you know . . ."

"Yes, yes—but I know, I can tell. It's going to be a bee-yootee-ful pic*tchah.*"

But, no soap: the contract was binding, there was nothing anyone could do. She would have to report for *The Subject Was Roses* on schedule. Pat was desolate and might well have been ruined for the picture if Roald hadn't taken a further downward turn that spelled immediate crisis and left no choice but to operate immediately. Once again in the life of the family the ambulance was called and two powerful attendants mounted the stairs to carry the sufferer away. Roald's size and weight made it a considerable chore to maneuver him down the narrow stairwell, and the pain of movement made him bite his lip hard to keep silent. Pat kissed the children good-bye and went out after him to ride into Oxford in the back of the ambulance. She was calm and in control of everything. "Listen, can you smoke in there?" she asked the driver, who laughed and told her that she could.

The first operation was a calamity, performed by the same surgeon who had been so luckless with Roald twenty-two years before. The offending cartilage was removed without difficulty, but the wound became septic and would not stop bleeding. Then Roald's neck went out again and he developed a fissure in the lower colon, making the whole length of his back a sea of pain and distress. Roald fought off all the drugs he could bear avoiding because he hated the woozy state of mind they induced. When the nurses insisted, he would put on his chief-surgeon's manner and calmly instruct them, "No, no, let me contramand the doctor's orders just this once and forgo the hypo. Do you mind?"

When Mumu died, Roald was too deeply engaged in his own survival to feel it very acutely. At least he showed what he might have felt only in a few words of regret that he hadn't been by her side. He had spoken to her on the telephone the day before, but he was unaware of how greatly she had slipped and had no sense of death being upon her. Pat, though, felt it very keenly and wept desperately at the funeral, which Roald could not attend. The coincidence of the spiritualized Mumu dying on the date of Olivia's death and having her service said in the same church and on the same day as Olivia's funeral seemed to chill Pat to the marrow.

"Do you know that it's seven years since bad things started happening to us? On December 5, it will be seven years since Theo was hit. If it's a seven-year curse, it better stop now, boy. These bad things better stop happening to us."

Roald's second operation corrected the first, and after nearly a month in the hospital he came home to Gipsy House, wearied and drastically subdued. His limp was more noticeable than Pat's, so that when they walked together and Pat was on his left side, their shoulders bumped every other step; when Pat was on the right they came apart at the top like calipers.

Pat was still reluctant to go to work on her movie and had been nursing the idea that perhaps Roald's health would not permit her leaving. But now there was no question of that, and Roald began making a few stabs at "jazzing Pat up."

"Do you want to hear my program for you, Pat? Exercise! I'm afraid a hundred and thirty-four on the scale doesn't mean much. Hardly better than a hundred and twenty-nine.

What you need is *muscle tone,* as it were. The old Marlene Dietrich formula. Have I ever told you how the Kraut keeps in such marvelous shape . . ."

But Pat had become a far more solid person during Roald's absence—Marjorie, the sisters, Tini and Joyce, everyone could see it, plain as day. There was a new air of purpose about her, and also a much strengthened confidence and will. She knew she had to start making *Roses* a month hence, and inconspicuously, she was beginning to prepare herself for it. All the same, it was a bleak time in the life of the family. The only good news December brought was that Theo had scored 97 in a mathematics quiz, putting him at the head of his class.

10

"LADIES AND GENTLEMEN, we've got a little gear situation here," said the captain's voice over the intercom. "It's nothing to be alarmed about, but we're not going to be landing on schedule here at National. We're going to be making a low pass over the field so the tower can confirm that our landing gear is down, and after that I'll advise you further."

"Well, I suppose that means we're all to be killed," Pat said lightly. She had arrived from England only the day before, and now she was with Lars McSorley, a bearded publicist hired by MGM to promote *The Subject Was Roses,* and myself, and we were on our way from New York to Washington, where President Johnson was to present Pat with the American Heart Association's Heart of the Year award on January 31. We were sitting in the horseshoe-shaped lounge at the back of the cabin, together with two

Germans, unknown to each other until garrulous Pat introduced them. "I think we *all* deserve a free martini," she said, and in a flash the stewardess was there with a tray.

"I'd like to propose a toast to you, and you, and you, and you—and to all the people we're leaving behind," Pat said with a devilish chuckle. She leaned over toward the two nervous Germans, a diplomat and an aeronautical engineer. "Do you have any children?" she asked. They gulped painfully and said yes. "How many?" They told her. "Too bad," she said in a grave voice that made everyone laugh.

"Folks, ladies and gentlemen," said the crackling loudspeaker voice. "We're not going to be landing at National this evening. We're turning back for Friendship, where the facilities are better."

"Oh, God," said Pat. Even if we live, we're going to be late for supper."

Lars scribbled notes, knowing that the least that could come of this crisis was a sure-fire column item. Already, after only one day at work, she had surpassed his wildest expectations, by giving two gay and witty press conferences, several radio and television interviews, and a long session with a writer from the *Saturday Evening Post*. Not only did everybody want to see her, she wanted to see everybody, and now she was even providing gallant, quotable gallows humor in the face of an air disaster.

"You aren't really worried, are you, babe?" Pat asked—a little nervously, I thought.

"Well, a little bit, Pat—yes, I am."

And I was. The stewardess had just announced what sounded disturbingly like crash-landing instructions (". . . gentlemen should loosen their neckties, and everyone be sure to remove glasses or pens or any sharp objects from their pockets") and the pilot had come on again to amend our destination to New York, "where the fire-fighting equipment is superior." The atmosphere inside the plane was becoming tense and prayerful.

"I'm not worried at all," Pat said. "Nothing scares me any more. I'm not even scared of meeting the President. If we survive, that is." She laughed a reckless laugh and called for another martini. The Germans were ashen and could only smile thinly when she raised her glass to them. "I was kidding when I said it was too bad you had so many children," she told them. "I have four of my own, not that their father couldn't take *splendid* care of them if I conked. But I'm sure we will survive. You'll see your children again. Have a drink and don't worry."

The passengers fell silent as the plane glided down into Kennedy Airport nearly three hours after it had taken off. It was as if everyone were listening for the first tiny sound of ripping metal, the whisper of the first exploding flames. Shirt collars were unbuttoned, eyes were closed, and a few seats up ahead a woman was holding an armful of pillows against her face. But there came only the life-giving thud of wheels brushing the runway, followed by a landing so gentle and smooth that the pessimists aboard felt a little sheepish for their fear. Pat shook hands all around, then joined the others as they shuffled up the aisle to the liberating draught of cold air at the door. "My compliments to the captain," she told the stewardess as she left the plane. "Tell him he did jolly well. And you're a beautiful woman, too."

Lars and I were a little uneasy about risking our lives on another plane right away, but Pat's only worry concerned the possibility of not getting to Washington in time for a good night's rest. "With my luck, you boys don't have a thing to worry about," she said, breaking into incongruous laughter. So we followed her onto a plane whose engines were racing, and an hour later we were safely at our destination.

"WAR'S WORST DAY" ran the headline in the Washington *Post* the morning that Pat was to meet the President. Knowing Pat's tendency to dismiss what she considered irrelevant, I went into her room in the Washington Hilton to warn her not to be disappointed if the White House canceled her out. The Vietnam war was only one of a large number of things that had occurred in the world since Pat had stopped caring; the day before, she had been flabbergasted to discover the nonchalance with which helicopters regularly took off and landed from the roof of a building in midtown Manhattan. But the prospect of the Tet offensive conflicting with the Heart of the Year award struck her as too remote to bother with, and she bore down instead on the need to think of something to say in acknowledgment. I wrote out a few lines for Pat to look over and she studied them under a hair drier, adding small grace notes until she had come up with what she wanted to say:

"My dear Mr. President. Thank you very much for this great honor. I feel especially good to be sharing it with you."

She ran the words over and over her tongue with increasing satisfaction. "Why do I say 'sharing it with you,' when he's really *giving* it to me?" she asked.

"Because he received the first award. He was the Heart of the Year in 1959."

Pat was aghast. "Did he have what I had?"

"No, he had a heart attack."

"Oh, that's a lot better," Pat said.

When it was time to leave and the White House still had not called to cancel the ceremony, Pat went down to the lobby to meet officials of the Heart Association, reciting her thank-you as if it were a mantra. Limousines were waiting. The Heart Association officers were terribly nervous during the ten-minute ride to the White House, but Pat calmed them or diverted their attention by asking how old they were, when their birthdays were, how many children they had. When the cars reached the White House and were passed through the gates to the west portico, Pat strained like the others to see everything going on inside.

Pat had forgotten to bring her passport, so she produced her Great Missenden checkbook by way of identification, but the Secret Service guard recognized her and got to his feet to usher her in. She went with the others to the Fish Room, with a promise of only a short wait.

Jesse Edwards, a St. Paul pathologist and president of the Heart Association, came over with his wife to soothe Pat's nerves, if needed. "Are you excited, Miss Neal?" he asked. "Just a little nervous?"

"You know, I'm really not," she said. "Nothing makes me nervous since this happened to me. It's not right."

Hubert Humphrey suddenly appeared in television make-up and made his way around the circle shaking hands.

"So very glad to meet *you*," he said to Pat, but his hand had already moved on to the next in line.

"My *dear* Mr. President . . . My *dear* Mr. President," Pat recited under her breath, moving away from the others. Marvin Watson, the President's appointments secretary, came in to explain the delay. "It's been a pretty tough morning, you know," he said with a diffident grin. "But you won't have to wait much longer. I'm really awfully sorry that you had to wait at all. I apologize."

"I accept," said Pat.

A Heart Association officer drifted over to amuse Pat with an anecdote: When Senator Lyndon Johnson received his award from President Eisenhower, relations were cool between them, and the ceremony was distant and chilly until Johnson broke the ice with a joke. After his heart attack, he said, when his condition was still critical, a call came from his tailor, where he had three suits on order; should he make them up or forget it, the tailor wanted to know. So Senator Johnson told Lady Bird, "Have him cancel the brown and the gray, but the blue will serve no matter what happens."

Pat laughed thinly at this, then asked, "Do *you* think it's all right for me to wear these green boots? He"—she gave me a mock glare—"thinks they're too informal and don't go with a blue dress."

"I think they look fine, Miss Neal. Very cheerful and nice."

"You better say that, because it's too late now."

And indeed it was: some unheard signal was siphoning the Fish Room empty. Pat followed the procession into the President's office. The President was standing by the door, looking old as winter, greeting each guest with a handshake, a heavy-lidded smile and a few whispered words; "It's good to seeya, good to seeya . . ."

When everyone was inside the oval office, some staff member said, "All right, gentlemen," and the room was suddenly awash with frantic photographers, fifty or more, working in perfect silence except for the locust buzz and clatter of their cameras. Klieg lights went on, seeming to cause the President to grow a foot and become frozen in a sixty-second smile. Dr. Edwards and Pat were steered to the President's side and the award, a silver plaque, materialized and was placed in the President's hands so that a pantomime presentation could be conducted for the press.

Then the aide said "Thank you, gentlemen," and the room instantly cleared; the photographers exited backward without a whimper of protest. President Johnson was left alone with the Heart Association party and half a dozen women reporters, whom he invited over to his desk to examine huge photographs of his grandson, inscribed with quips by Luci Baines: "And when I'm elected, I promise a full bottle in every crib"; "Who am I voting for? I'm *running.*" There seemed to be about seventy-five pictures in all, and after several uncomfortable minutes of waiting on the fringe of the crowd, Dr. Edwards got the idea that the fake presentation had been the real one and that everyone was supposed to leave.

"No, no," his wife scolded. "It will take all the dignity away from the award if it isn't properly presented. You stayed up all night working on your speech. Now give it." Dr. Edwards drew a deep breath, stepped forward, and more or less tugged at the President's jacket. Mr. Johnson turned sharply.

"Mr. President," the doctor said in a loud rostrum voice, "each year the American Heart Association singles out one American . . ." The President resigned himself to giving up the baby pictures. He listened intently as the speech ran on. ". . . her faith, courage and achievement in meeting the personal challenge of cardiovascular disease have inspired people everywhere with new hope and the determination to conquer our nation's leading health enemy . . ."

The President's response was spoken so softly that one had to strain to hear it. "I guess you're as grateful as I am for the science that made it possible for you and me to be here together," he said. Pat nodded emphatically. "And I must say that the appearance of the recipients of these awards has certainly improved." Excessive laughter filled the room; Pat was beaming beautifully. Then the President embarked on a strange monologue, describing the epic portion of "crisis" that fate had served up to him ("Medical crises, political crises, military crises, economic crises") and observing that a great many people who would normally ignore you take a sudden interest when the roof caves in. This led into a retelling of the tailor story, which in the context seemed to suggest that the tailor ("my little tailor, Joe") was, like the "pressmen and photographers," a hungry, circling vulture, waiting for the king to fall. The story trailed off in muted laughter, and the ceremony was over.

Pat didn't get a chance to give her little speech.

⚙

"All right, bells! And . . . roll 'em . . ."

"Scene 35, take 26. *The Subject Was Roses.*" Slap of the clapboard.

". . . and action!"

The set stood in the middle of the sound stage, a Bronx apartment laid back and dissected under a galaxy of floodlights and spots that probed in through its absent ceiling. The art director had done his work so well that a walk through the fake apartment was bewitching, even for the actors and crew. The worn furniture and blistered paint bespoke many humdrum years within the collapsible walls, and the quality of light that streamed through the empty windows made it difficult to realize that half an inch beyond them was the dim warehouse studio with its silent staff of technicians and grips, its elaborate array of equipment, and the sargasso of power and light cables curling all over the floor.

The three actors did nothing to dispel the impression that the apartment was the true living quarters of a middle-class Irish family in the Bronx. Jack Albertson in tweed topcoat and limp fedora was John Cleary, pious, frustrated, philandering coffee broker, going off to work. Martin Sheen was Timmy, John's son, just home from the war, tormented by his first adult perception of his parents' estrangement. And there by the sink, in housedress and kitchen apron, stood Pat, who as John's wife, Nettie, had measured out her disappointment in a thousand silent hours at that sink.

"You know I can't," Albertson said, picking up the action on a cue from Ulu Grosbard, the director. Even in his director's campaign chair and with a viewfinder hanging from a cord around his neck, Ulu still looked like a young violinist. *"This thing with Ruskin means a sure sale."*

"I understand," said Martin Sheen, playing the line for

the weighted indifference of a sensitive son catching his father in a con.

"We'll go tomorrow," said Albertson, with the concluding lilt of a man with a bus to catch.

"But we're meant to have supper— God damn it! JESUS! I can't get this line!"

"Cut!" shouted Ulu, crossing the set to have a word with his star.

Pat was miserable. A week of rehearsal and six days of shooting had produced no disaster like this—twenty-six takes of the same stupid scene and she didn't have the line right yet. *"My mother expects us for dinner tomorrow."* That was all there was to it, but every time her cue arrived, imposter words would intervene; instead of producing the line as it was written, her traitor brain would offer old formula phrases, relics of her illness. "We're meant to go to supper." Or "I'm very sorry to tell you. . . ." Or else a desperate, gagging silence that left her biting the air and forced gentle Ulu to cry "Cut!" once again. They talked quietly in a corner of the kitchen, with Pat nodding continuously at everything Ulu said. She was a professional actress, and it showed, even in despairing moments.

The next time around, Pat got the line right and the three actors breezed through another ten lines before Ulu cut the scene and shouted "Print!" Cheers went up from all corners of the room, causing Pat to burst into happy laughter and bow from the waist, saying, "Thank you, thank you, I thank you, my fans." Then she retreated to her dressing room, shadowed by Val, who was serving as secretary, helper and script coach. Val had been urging all along that Pat curtail other activities in an all-out assault on the script, but now

Pat told her to sit down and lectured her sternly about the need for Val to keep reminding her of the work that was still undone.

"I *cannot* keep going out to supper every night," Pat said. "It's got to stop."

"Well, yes, Pat, that's what I've sort of meant to be suggesting." Val could take on the manner of a wet blanket proved right at moments like this, but Pat was too involved with her new determination to take much notice. Her fear of not knowing her lines had defeated her will to work up until the very moment of beginning, as if deep within her she was resolved not to test the limits of her capacities; if she failed and could write it off to laziness, the setback would be easier to bear than if failure came after she had given her best effort. Now, having actually gotten through the first few scenes, her energy was released to make dramatic amends for long months of inattention to her work. Her commitment was fierce: she wanted to work, and no more nonsense about it.

Lars McSorley cruised in just as Pat was telling Val that they had to cut back on all the interviews—a point Val had made many times before.

"Why have you got those dark glasses on?" Pat demanded at the sight of McSorley's face at the door.

"I was out rather late last night," he answered in a morning voice.

"Take 'em off. Let me see," said Pat.

"No, no, I'd rather just—"

"Take 'em off, boy, I want to see." She reached out to grab them off his nose. McSorley dodged, then slid the glasses down like a coroner displaying a corpse.

"Aaaggghhh!" Pat screamed. "Put 'em back on again. That's terrible! You must have got *so-o-o-o* drunk last night."

"Well, yes, a few glasses were raised."

"You better cut it out, boy, or you'll kill yourself."

"Maybe I just better go out and come in all over again."

"Do that," said Pat, and when he entered again, Pat plugged him with the other barrel: "Listen—aaahhh . . . *Lars,* we've *got* to cut out some of these interviews. I can't do it. I had to do a scene over . . . how many times was it, Val?"

"Twenty-seven."

"Twenty-seven times! I must work harder on my script and I can't do it if there's always another interview. And you know that my husband's coming over next week?"

McSorley nodded. She had told him several times, in fact —each time not precisely in the form of a question but rather as a confirmation that everyone knew the password to her excitement. It was a question that became a reminder in midsentence, with Pat's whole look and tone changing as she spoke, the curious raised eyebrow becoming instead the bridge to a half wink that said, "Yes, you know; you've got it, kiddo."

"Well, Pat, there're quite a few interviews already set up. Do you want me to cancel them?"

"No, don't cancel any. Just don't arrange too many more. Who's coming to see me?" She listened in intently as McSorley ran through the names. This was a tonic for her: to think how famous she was. Her earlier visits to New York and Los Angeles had not fully revealed the adulation in which she was held, and she had not in the least anticipated it. When Roald called her "the poor man's Jacqueline Kennedy," she didn't give it much weight, and not even the houseful of plaques and awards she had received in the past three years had convinced her of her status or shown her its fantastic, embracing dimensions. But now there were signs of it everywhere. The Paragon Greenhouses, she had just heard, had named a new hybrid rose "The Patricia Neal."

LISTEN, PAPA [she wrote home to Roald], I HATE TO TELL YOU BUT I AM VERY FAMOUS HERE NOW. IT PLEASES ME. LAST NIGHT I WENT TO SUPPER WITH ULU, MY DIRECTOR, AT A FINE RESTAURANT. WE TALKED AND TALKED WHICH MEANS WE KNOW EACH OTHER BETTER. AND ULU IS A DIVINE MAN AND A GREAT DIRECTOR. BUT WHAT I CAN'T TELL YOU IS HOW GOOD THEY WERE TO ME, THOSE RESTAURANT MEN. AND I'M THRILLED WITH WHAT HAPPENED AT SARDI'S TONIGHT. A MAN CAME OVER AND TOLD HOW MUCH HE LOVES YOUR STORIES AND HIS SON'S LOVE OF YOUR CHILDREN'S BOOKS. THAT COMPLIMENTS YOU DOESN'T IT?

Pat read the children's letters aloud to Lily, her hairdresser; Mike, the make-up man; Val; me; anyone who happened to be around.

"Now I come to think I am a terrible daughter. I have woken up at last. But you *must* think what marvellous parents we are. Buying such lovely things for our NO GOOD DAUGHTER. Paying her school fees when she has know Brain to think with. The conclusion should be WE SHOULD BE PROUD OF OUR SELF'S. OH, MAMA & PAPA, YOU BOTH HAVE GREAT RIGHT TO BE JOLLY JOLLY PROUD OF YOUR SELF'S. So please send me my needs (ha ha). Thanks tons for putting up with me.

"Love,
"TESSA"

"How are you? We are fine. Don't forget to get Theo a Action Man.

"We are staying at Marjorie's house tonight. Could you bring Michael a tommy gun?

"How are you getting on in America? We went to see Theo's teacher and she told us to get away. Theo wants to go and visit one of our teachers who lives in Flat 6. Theo wants to clean her car for her.

"Love,
"THEO AND MICHAEL"

From Ophelia (as told to Tini):

"Is Mummy fine? Is Mummy very fine in New York? I love Mummy so much. I hope she comes back forever and ever. I like Mummy about 120 weeks. A lot. I hope Mummy is fine. When she comes back she thinks she likes herself. She talks to Val, talking loud in the aeroplane. Val loves Mummy about 100. She will come back and I will give her some soap.

"Love,
"OPHELIA"

"I love to give presents.
"I want to give you soap.
"I love to give you a present.
"I love to give you a prize.
"Thank you very much for having me.
"I love to give you a kiss.
"I love to sit on the table.
"I love Mummy 100.

"Love,
"LUCY"

The letters completed the circuit of Pat's happiness; even Roald's came addressed to "My darling Pat," and were more tender than Roald could ever be in speech. Better still, his news was good. He was feeling strong and spirited and was riding a fine winning streak at the blackjack tables in London. Pat showed off the letters together with pictures of Roald and the children much as a soldier might do at the front. The "great maternal surge" Roald had been predicting since Lucy's birth was upon her with a passion, three thousand miles from home. It showed in the way she met new people, interrogating them about their families, wanting to know every child's name and age. She was torn between ecstasies—her family, her friends, the film, the great adoring crowd of reporters and headwaiters.

Things were running so smoothly by the time Roald arrived that he became immediately contentious. Appearances to the contrary, it was obvious that Pat could not be having such a good time without it hurting her work. "What time have you been getting up, approximately?" he asked on his first night in town, waiting to unleash his disapproving lecture on the sin of rising at noon.

"It's been six-forty-five just about every morning," Val said.

"Five-thirty once," Pat added.

"So you're napping in the afternoons, are you?"

"Napping. Listen, babe, we're working. You're the one who can take naps now."

All Roald's jabs were parried until he could only admit to being impressed. "I'll have to spend an afternoon at the studio," he said, salvaging a bit of ground.

"You won't believe what you see," Val said. "I promise you."

Neither Pat nor Roald had ever seemed concerned that the damage to Pat's brain would injure her talent itself. Pat was obsessed with her loss of memory, Roald with her judgment and morale, but neither questioned the survival of the delicate properties that were uniquely hers—the system of empathies and the gifts of expression that made her Patricia Neal. Roald had even suggested that the stroke would deepen her art by enlarging her range of experience, much as Olivia's death and Theo's accident had. "These young actresses have to invent everything," he would say. "They haven't lived enough to draw on their own lives for the things they're supposed to feel onstage. When you see a really good one, a top actress like Pat, you'll find every time that she's someone who's been through it." Pat did not argue with this, but she made no predictions of her own. She merely assumed that if she could get the lines right, she'd be as good as ever.

Early in the shooting, it seemed that they had been too optimistic. For even when Pat had her lines down cold, she sometimes failed to locate the precise tonality of voice or gesture to express a nuance of feeling. It was as if she were having trouble understanding the implications of the words the script called for. The problem paralleled the last subtle symptom of her asphasia, which was also a question of tonalities: she knew what she thought, she knew what she felt, but the words she found to express herself were often much too large or too small. People were either "gr-r-reat" and "heavenly" and "divine" or else "rotten"; she either "loved" things or "hated" them, no matter how trivial they were.

But as Pat got into her role and became comfortable again in the atmosphere of a sound stage, the cameras seemed to work magic on her. She went to work in a happier frame of mind than most people can muster before dawn, and while the hairdresser and make-up man worked on her, she ran through her lines with a depth of concentration that delighted Roald when he saw it. "You'd hardly recognize the old Beatrix Potter fan, would you?" he said as he sat on the couch in her snug little dressing room, watching the actress prepare.

"Quiet, you two!" Pat said, then turned back to Val, who held the soft green book that contained Pat's script, all underlined and annotated in Valerie's careful hand. "Now, I say, *'Here—I'll do it,'* and what does he say?"

"He says, *'Did you ever see such pretty hair?'* "

Pat nodded. Right! said the glint in her eye.

" *'Will you please let me open this door?'* " She spoke the line with a kind of resigned content that projected the sense of a woman accustomed to coming home with a slightly drunken husband at the end of an evening that had flattered and amused her. The hint of good-humored impatience was exactly right for the scene.

"Then Timmy says, *'Beautiful hair,'* " Val recited, "and you unlock the door, and John says, *'Home to wife and mother.'* "

"That's right. And I turn the lights on and say, *'Someday we'll break our necks because you refuse to leave a light.'* It isn't supposed to be *'leave a light on'*?" Pat looked around to Roald for an answer, causing the make-up man to shrink back nervously with his lip brush.

"It says *'leave a light,'* Pat," said Val.

"Then *'leave a light'* it is," Pat said firmly, reaching out for her cold cup of coffee. Mike drew back again.

"The only problem you have working with Pat," he said to the room at large, "is that you've got to hit a moving target."

Pat laughed gaily and settled back to let Mike finish her make-up.

That afternoon, with Roald watching from the wings, Pat and Jack Albertson ran through half a dozen takes of the film's one violent scene, in which the husband makes an awkward pass at his indifferent wife and tears her blouse open in the process—"the rape scene," as Pat called it. "I hate to have to tell you what he's going to do to me," she told Roald as she went on.

The scene began with a quiet rejection. *"One nice evening doesn't make everything different,"* Pat said as the camera rolled in tight for a close-up.

"Did I say it did?" Jack came up behind her and lightly kissed the nape of her neck. The kiss seemed to chill and frighten her. Her voice became apprehensive, tinged with a note of disgust.

"That's perfect, Pat," said Ulu, breaking in on the scene to make another adjustment in the way the actors stood before the camera. A half step forward. Perhaps an inch or two to the right. The bell rang, the clapboard was struck, the cameras rolled, the actors started again from the top.

"It's marvelous how she can do it over and over again and

keep coming up with the same emotion, isn't it?" Roald said. He was leaning against a screen of two-by-fours that supported the wall to the room, puffing at his pipe and looking on with an unusually obvious show of pride.

"She seems as good as ever," I said.

"Easily," Roald said with a connoisseur's assurance. "It's all come back to her now."

When Pat came off the set after the scene had been run through for the last time, Roald greeted her with his pride-and-embarrassment chuckle. "You're really in your element, aren't you?" he teased, intending a restrained compliment.

"Well, what do you *think?* Do you like it? Am I any good?"

"Marvelous," said Roald. "Really quite marvelous." He chuckled again in the same bashful way. Then, in full public view, he put his arm around her shoulders and walked with her to her dressing room. It was a rare, rare moment, for me as well as them; in all the time I had known them I had never seen Roald get so mushy.

Pat became more and more commanding as the shooting wore on. There were scenes to be shot on location in the Bronx, in downtown Manhattan, in a Greenwich Village bar, on the New Jersey coast, as well as the grinding day-in, day-out sessions at the studio. But nothing shook her composure or discouraged her or even seemed to tire her very much. She and Val ate most of their suppers in their hotel room and Pat was often in bed by nine. She hardly needed the alarm clock to wake her, and some mornings she was up and ready for work so early that she had time to write a letter home before a quarter to seven, when the chauffeur rang.

The hard work and disciplined schedule would have been oppressive and defeating to her six months before, but now she was thriving on them. It showed in her face, in her humor and in the immediate, almost childlike pleasure she found in being able to live up to the picture's demands. "I *love* Ulu," she would say, "and I think he is pleased with me. Yesterday he said he thought I was jolly good."

She did not seem to be especially interested in the character she was playing—an inward, permanently cheated woman, whose hopeful beginnings and disappointing marriage have made her a dishpan martyr, especially to herself. This was a woman totally unlike Pat, a woman without Pat's humor or courage or humility, without her capacity for either life or love. Pat did not despise her or fail to sympathize with her sufferings; she simply avoided talking much about her, and she gave the impression of never thinking very deeply about her when the day's work was done. Pat may have been an Actors Studio graduate, but her performance had nothing to do with the Method. She made no attempt to *be* the person she was playing except in front of the cameras.

Near the end of the picture Pat had several long monologues, which had terrified her from the start. It was one thing to be able to tick off the short, conversational speeches, and quite another to get through a couple of hundred words in scenes that had to be done in a single take. But by the time these passages were ready to be shot, Pat had regained the knack for memorizing lines, or at least the better part of it. She stumbled and broke the action on forgotten words, but less often than any number of other actresses might have done. Marilyn Monroe, who was notorious for her poor memory, was often invoked as a kind of reverse inspiration: "Marilyn would have taken twice as long, Pat"; "If you think you're bad, you should have seen Marilyn."

Pat's example and her effusive warmth touched the entire cast and crew, and by the time she was finished with her part in the production, everyone had become convinced that the picture they were making was a great one, an Oscar winner perhaps. Pat was completely credulous of all the self-congratulatory talk. "Do you think there's really a chance of an Oscar?" she asked all comers. And it was clear from the look in her eye that she was determined to believe that there was.

When she left for home, Pat gave everyone in the company a copy of one of Roald's books, autographed by her. Work stopped early that day and Ulu presided over a farewell party at which great amounts of champagne were poured. Pat had made friends with nearly everyone on the set, and her departure was taken rather hard by some. There were tears, hugs, kisses: actors saying good-bye leave very little unsaid. The cast and crew had chipped in to buy her a farewell present, a silver-and-coral pin in the form of a rose, and she wore it like a badge on her collar the night her plane took off. The next morning's papers carried a bulletin saying that her plane had arrived in London trailing fire from one engine, but Pat said later that it was really nothing. She hadn't even noticed it, in fact.

✿

"She's looking wonderful, really wonderful," said the elevator operator in Pat's hotel. "She looks a lot better than she did when she was here before."

I had not seen Pat since she left New York after the picture was finished, nearly six months before. Now she was back for its premiere. I couldn't imagine that she would look very different from the triumphant woman I had last seen waving from the ramp of a plane. Roald and I had exchanged letters, and he had reported nothing more dramatic than a change of cooks, a new school for Tessa, a couple of passing illnesses, plans for new construction at Gipsy House. Only a few weeks before, a letter had come saying that Pat was riding almost too high: "Pat's been queening it around the place ever since she came home. Yesterday evening she was upstairs dressing for some charity with Princess Alexandra and she yelled down the stairs, 'ROALD! Can't you hear me? I said I wanted a martini up here!' As you can imagine, I gave her what-for."

The picture of Roald climbing the stairs with a few well-chosen words instead of a martini was warmly familiar, and I had expected to find Pat in all ways unchanged. For at least two years her recovery had been a subtle, patient process, and while watching her at work on the film, I had grown to think that it was finally complete. A few signs of the stroke still remained, but one had to know her well to catch a glimpse of them.

The elevator reached Pat's floor and I walked down the hall and knocked at the door to her suite.

"Well, *hello-o-o,* baby!" Pat said, flinging the door open hard and pulling me inside.

I could see right away what the elevator operator meant. She looked abundantly healthy and alive, dressed in red, wearing her rose, smiling her wide-screen smile. I stood back to take her in and she drew a deep breath and struck a happy pose. The change that had come over her was very slight; perhaps it was that her smile now included her eyes in a way it hadn't before.

Pat had not seen the movie and she grilled me relentlessly on the way to a screening Ulu had arranged for her. Was she horrible? Was she great? Who was best? Would anyone get an Oscar? But when the screening room fell dark and filled with the film's haunting music and a full-screen image of Pat's face, she relaxed into a fine, accepting calm that didn't leave her until the lights went up again. The only scenes she remarked about were a few where one could detect a tiny clue to her condition: a shot in which her limp showed, another where she held a water pitcher in her right hand and let her index finger stand out rigidly instead of curling around the handle. Beyond that, she had no criticism of herself or anyone else. She liked it and was proud of it and needed no one's reassurance.

The premiere was like any other, except for a superb portrait of Pat that flashed in moving lights on the Acutron sign over Broadway. There were spotlights on the sidewalk, limousines drawing up, photographers pushing against the velvet ropes, a long-stemmed Patricia Neal Rose for all the ladies. Roald had come over from England for the occasion just that afternoon and was unsettled by the plane ride and the loss of sleep.

"Fantastic nonsense, isn't it?" he said, twisting through the crowd to get out of photographer's range. "I hate these bloody things, but Pat is in her glory, so we mustn't say a word. Look at her over there. She's *loving* it. She can't get enough of it." He stood tall to see over the crowd and threw back his head in the prideful chuckle when Pat saw him and waved.

It was difficult to sustain the excitement once the movie began. Its melancholy became the mood of the audience, and a hush lay over the theater that was broken only by a few moments of grateful laughter—all in the right places. The strength of the film was in the performances, and it was Pat's, the least embellished of the three, that gave it a depth and clarity that ennobled the others and made the slender story count. There was a full-hearted round of applause at the end and many in the audience appeared to have been crying as they headed up the aisle.

The reviews were superlative "12 Roses and One Thorn," as the ad on the movie page had it. Pat's old nemesis, the *New York Times,* roasted the movie for its sentimentality and lack of importance, but the praise for Pat was unanimous. Many of the critics made a point of discounting the tremendous distance she had come to give a performance at all, judging her only as an actress and finding her sublime.

Pat was leaving for Hollywood on an afternoon plane and Roald wanted to get back home to the nippers that night. Even so, they had time to go through the thick stack of clippings MGM sent up for Pat to see. Roald read them to himself at first, shaking his head and laughing.

"What's so funny?" Pat asked. "Read it aloud."

"Oh, it's just some love-struck journalist raving on about you."

"Well, read it!"

Roald smiled broadly to himself and went on to the next. He read the whole column while Pat drank coffee and watched his face for reactions. At length he looked up and nodded gravely, indicating deep agreement.

"This is *Time,*" he said. "They say that your performance would be worth waiting a decade for. They say, '. . . she doesn't portray suffering, she defines it.' Rather good, you know. Marvelous."

"A gr-r-reat critic wrote that," Pat said with happy conviction. "Read it to me again . . ."

ABOUT THE AUTHOR

Barry Farrell was born and raised in Washington State and received his B.A. from the University of Washington at Seattle, where he was also a Woodrow Wilson Fellow. Since then he has lived and worked in San Francisco, New York, Paris and Haiti, holding a number of varied jobs, including political speech writer, newspaper reporter and teacher. For several years he was a correspondent and writer for *Time* and *Life,* and it was on a *Life* assignment in the summer of 1965 that Mr. Farrell first met Patricia Neal and Roald Dahl. He is now a columnist for *Life* magazine.